BLUE EYESHADOW
SHOULD BE ILLEGAL

Still

BLUE EYESHADOW
SHOULD BE ILLEGAL

Still

The World After Retin-A: What Do You Do Now?

by Paula Begoun

REVISED AND UPDATED 1988

Art Direction: Constance Bollen
Cover Design: Art Attack & Constance Bollen
Typography: Michael Hofferbert, Common Line
Copy Editing: Shellie Tucker
Printing: R.R. Donnelley

Copyright 1988 by Paula Begoun
10 9 8 7 6 5 4 3 2

Publisher: Beginning Press
          5418 South Brandon
          Seattle, Washington 98118

This book may be ordered directly from the publisher:
5418 South Brandon
Seattle, Washington 98118

Dedication

My dear friend Julie has shared her wisdom and love with me during the past several years, over many fresh-brewed cups of morning coffee. Through her special language of acceptance and joy I have learned that the blush of laughter is the most beautiful fashion look of all.

Acknowledgments

To my mother-in-law, Sarah Bush, for being a good sport and a great cook, my sister-in-law Liz Rosen for being patient and sincerely supportive, my husband for not complaining too much as I sat downstairs writing until all hours of the morning, and to all the women who have written and thanked me for writing the original version of *Blue Eyeshadow*. It was always a welcome breath of fresh air every time I opened one of your letters letting me know that there really was someone listening.

With Special Thanks

Dr. Albert Kligman, the inventor of Retin-A, called me moments before I sent this book off to be typeset with a few suggestions about how to improve my manuscript. After we discussed those changes he quietly added that the information in the skin-care section was well-done and easy to read. I greatly appreciate Dr. Kligman for taking time out of his busy schedule to offer advice and improvements. It also felt affirming that he tossed in a compliment at the same time.

Professional Thank Yous

Special professional thank yous to: photographer David Hagyard for his consistently brilliant photography, hair designer Robbe from the Ambiance Salon in Seattle for his skill and talent and Constance Bollen for her delightful interior design of this book.

Table of Contents

Chapter 1: What's All The Confusion About?
Why The Confusion?   16
About The Author   20

Chapter 2: A Cosmetic Quiz — Flights of Advertising Fantasy
Quiz 1 — Examine Your Makeup Attitudes   26

Chapter 3: The Cinderella Myth
Being Realistic About Cosmetics   34
To Correct Or Not To Correct?   35
Beauty Is A Dated Word   38
Being Realistic About Yourself   40
Brand-Name Addiction   41
A New Wrinkle In Skin-Care Promises   44
Advertising: Fact Or Fiction?   44

**Chapter 4: Skin Care — And Now For Something
          That Is Still Completely Different**
Quiz 2 — Face Facts   50
Skin Care From The Outside In   55
Forget Skin Type?!   56
But Don't Forget Sensitive Skin   59
Finally, Let's Clean The Face   60
Find A Good Water-Soluble Cleanser   62
Stress, Inflammation and Irritation   64
No Bar Soap!   66
No More Astringents   68
To Slough Or Not To Slough?   70
Clearing The Oil Panic!   72
Twisted Logic   74
After The Cleanser — Step Two   74
After Step Two — Step Three   77
You Want Me To Use Milk Of Magnesia Where?   79
Everyday Normal Facial Masks   81
Understanding Acne And Blackheads   82
Acne Myth #1   84
Acne Myth #2   85

Doctoring The Skin   86
Growing Up With Acne   87
After The Days Of Accutane   89
Retin-A For Acne   91
Cleocin Lotion   94
What To Ask Your Doctor   95
A Just-In-Case Checklist   97

Chapter 5: The World After Retin-A
I Told You So   100
Face Up To The Truth   102
Dry Skin Vs. Wrinkles — Separating The Evidence
    From The Process   105
Genetic Aging Vs. Photoaging   106
Miscellaneous Wrinkling   109
One More Time — THE SUN WARNING   110
I Almost Forgot — This Is Step Five   113
What's In That Stuff?   115
Water, Oil And Wax — The Real Secret Ingredients   116
Collagen — Yesterday's News   118
Reading Between The Lines   119
To Lift Or Not To Lift?   121
Filling In The Lines   123
Collagen Injections   124
Retin-A: What Do You Do Now?   125
Retin-A: The Story   126
What It Really Does   127
Before You Start   128
After You Start   129
Smooth Sailing   130
How Long Is The Treatment?   131
What Happened To Me   134
Questions And Answers   137
Skin-Care-Guide Summary   140
A Few Quick Comments — Comparison Shopping   142
Speaking Of Ingredients   143
Allergic Reactions   144
Drug Vs. Cosmetic   145

Hair Removal 146
Liposomes 148
Skin Care On Television 150

**Chapter 6: Assessing Who You Are And How That
Affects Your Makeup**
A Personality & Image Profile Test 152
The Results 156
Personality and Makeup 159
How We Handle Change 161
Dress Your Face According To Your Image 161
Image Characteristics 163
Image Theory 167
Putting The Two Tests Together 168

Chapter 7: A New Beginning For You And Your Makeup
A Quick But Honest Introduction 172
Before You Start 173
Never Do More Than You Have To! 175
Highlighting — Making Dark Look Light 177
Types Of Highlighters 179
Foundation 182
Matching Skin Color 186
An Exception To The Rule 188
Types of Foundation 189
Powdering 193
Brushes 194
Contouring 197
Under The Cheekbone 199
Sides Of The Nose 200
Temple Contour 201
Blushing 202
Eyeshadow Application 203
Designing The Eye 204
Back Wedge 208
U-shaped Crease 210
True Crease 213
Eyeliners 214
Drippies 216

Mascara 217

Blue Eyelashes? 219

Eyebrows 220

Lipstick And Lipliner 223

How Much Makeup? 226

Matching Your Makeup To Your Personality 226

Chapter 8: The Last Hurdle

Choosing Colors That Work 230

The Agony And The Ecstasy — Choosing Color 232

What If My Clothes Are The Wrong Color? 233

Is Fashion Awareness For Everyone? 233

Blue Eyeshadow Should Still Be Illegal! 234

A Quick Review 235

Potential Problems 236

What To Do If You Wear Glasses 238

Chapter 9: Miscellaneous Touches

How To Shop For Makeup 240

Judging The Texture Of A Powder 240

What's In A Name? 241

Put My Blush Where? 241

Makeup Bags — A Holding Tank 242

Where Do You Put On Your Makeup? 242

Cosmetic Acne 242

Choosing A Makeup Artist 243

What To Discuss With Your Makeup Artist 244

How To Deal With Cosmetic Salespeople 245

They're Out To Get Our Children 246

The Final Word — Makeup And Sexuality 248

Recommended Reading 251

Why Do I Still Call This Book, Blue Eyeshadow Should Be Illegal?

When I first wrote all this down three years ago, I knew that somewhere someone, if not everyone, was going to react to the title, which fortunately they did. After two quick years and a few dozen talk shows later, there were over 100,000 copies sold. The letters that thanked me for writing a truly unique book about the cosmetic industry came in almost every day, which made my ego feel great. That's not to say there weren't letters that reacted unfavorably to the title. There were those who rebuked me for my foolishness, lack of awareness and good taste. (Thank goodness I only received a handful of those.) My strongest critics accused me of being jealous or having never met any blonde-haired, blue-eyed women. Didn't I know that women with blonde hair and blue eyes all look wonderful in blue eyeshadow? Several men shrugged their shoulders and looked at me like, what's the big deal, and then they would say, "This isn't exactly a political or environmental issue is it? I like it when my wife wears blue eyeshadow." The most surprising response was from my mother-in-law, who, on occasion, wears greyblue eyeshadow and lines the inner rim of her eyes in black, hoping that I won't notice. Well, I always notice except I only say something if someone else brings up the subject of makeup application first and she happens to be in the room blatantly rimmed in black and framed in blue. (That's okay Mom, I love you no matter what color eyeshadow you wear.) The difference between this book and the original is my approach to the whole subject of skin care and cosmetics. In some instances I've taken a less radical stand and in others I have become more adamant. As far as content goes there are more detailed explanations to help clarify why I recommend one skin-care item over another and why I want you to throw many of them away. I've also included several quizzes designed to help you take a closer look at how you perceive your image, skin, makeup and knowledge about cosmetics. The one area I really enjoyed expanding on was debunking the never-ending "look younger too" advertising hoaxes that continue to haunt us in the media. The most interesting thing I did for this update was to personally experience several types of minor medical/cosmetic procedures so I could share with you what they were like. For professional and personal reasons I was more than just a little curious to try collagen injections, Retin-A and the like before this book went to press.

The major difference in this updated version of *Blue Eyeshadow* is indicated by the new subtitle, *The World After Retin-A: What Do You Do Now?* I'm sure there aren't many women out there who haven't heard or read about this 1988 version of the fountain of youth. How Retin-A affects the way we look at the world of skin care and sun-damaged skin is incredibly significant and yet, as you might have suspected, there is a trade-off. Retin-A has some side effects that you need to know about and definitely need to know how to handle if you're going to jump on the bandwagon and discover for yourself if Retin-A really can tackle your wrinkles. This edition of *Blue Eyeshadow* will lay out step by step what to expect, how you can get started safely, and what you can do if you run into problems once you begin Retin-A therapy.

The reason for renaming this book *Blue Eyeshadow Should Still Be Illegal* is because my original sentiment is still valid — I believe blue eyeshadow, even if only symbolically, is a mistake women create with their makeup: namely, overcoloring their lids, unwittingly allowing the shadow or eyepencil color to be more noticeable than their eyes! The symbolic mistake is that women are not being objective about how they look at themselves, and the cosmetic industry. I base that on the following logic: Blue eyeshadow is the number-one-selling cosmetic color. The major reason women buy makeup is because of the misleading information that abounds in the world of makeup and skin care. Something has to be wrong when so many women are buying and wearing blue eyeshadow. That same logic follows for wrinkle creams, astringents and on and on . . . Unless we do something different about the way we buy makeup, the cosmetic industry is going to continue to lead us around the proverbial merry-go-round, that never-ending circle of packaged promises costing between $2.00 and $75.00 a pop.

Blue Eyeshadow Should Still Be Illegal is not a book that will teach you how to mix eggwhites with avocados or oatmeal with honey to use on any part of the face to get it clean. (You've been led to believe that natural and good are equal and that is not true!) This book will also NOT have you go through a lengthy cosmetic routine of toner, moisturizer, eye cream, blemish cover, skin color corrector, highlighter, foundation and powder. You will not be told that moisturizers *protect* the skin from other makeup or that eye creams are specially designed for the eye area or that the foundation must be applied all over, because none of that is true. If those are the things you want, there are plenty of books and magazines offering that, but not this one. This time you will get alternatives that offer a short-cut to the exact same destination.

As I have stated before, this isn't a hot domestic topic, like pollution or the national debt. There are *worse* things than wearing blue, bright lime-green or shiny rose-pink eyeshadows. Rather it is a personal issue that most women share in common. The issue is, how much money are we willing to waste at the cosmetic counters? It's still a good question because, unfortunately, we're still wasting money.

This new, revised edition of *Blue Eyeshadow Should Still Be Illegal* will provide updated information and answer the questions I have been asked most frequently. This book is a compilation of what I have been teaching, reporting on and discussing over the past ten years. I know you will find some, if not all, of the contents to be interesting and helpful. If nothing else, I promise it will be different and entertaining.

Paula Begoun

Chapter One
What's All The Confusion About?

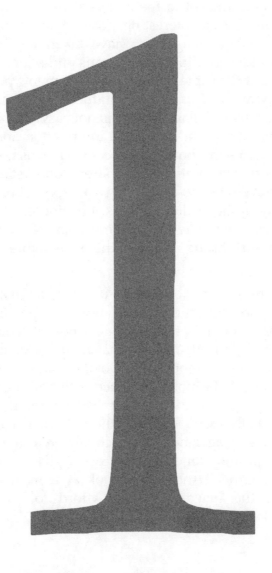

Why The Confusion?

The makeup and skin-care routines, both expensive and inexpensive, as advertised and packaged by thousands of cosmetic lines all over the world, have placed women in an interesting position of noninformation saturation. Fashion magazines have taken the business of beauty and reduced it to clever slogans and scientific mumbo jumbo while at the same time reducing women's pocketbooks and objectivity. Resisting media-induced ideas as skillfully created by a billion-dollar industry is not easy. To be an aware consumer takes a lot of solid, real information and courage. Information, from this book's perspective, means honest, practical and easy explanations that stress understanding and usage. Courage refers to assertively asking questions, not taking anything at face value and, last but not least, looking at the entire cosmetic issue from a new point of view. But first you need to sort through some of the mess before you can do that.

There are three major sources of information available to the public concerning the makeup industry. One of the most accessible are articles in fashion magazines. Millions of these magazines peer out at us from magazine racks all over the country. Month after month they boldly headline new insight into the secrets of fashion excellence. After all these millions of issues I am overwhelmed at the meager amount of information that actually exists between the front and back covers. Although these magazines don't actually lie to the consumer about makeup and skin-care, they don't give the reader the entire truth, either. And if you look at it from a business perspective, the magazines can't afford to. Let's take a hypothetical situation as an example:

Imagine you are the editor of a major fashion magazine. Your circulation is seven-million copies distributed monthly. Besides the subscription sales and the newsstand sales your major source of consistent revenue are your advertisers. The fashion designers, cosmetic companies, liquor companies, and food companies, Lord bless them, pay hundreds of thousands of dollars a year to reach your readers. Their prime target: upscale women between 25 and 55 looking to improve their position in life. Great business so far, isn't it?

Think about that scenario for a minute. Now consider that a young, or not so young, enthusiastic consumer specialist comes along and wants to do a series of articles to inform your readers how the cosmetic industry is trying to pull the wool over their wrinkles. You read the articles and they have a lot of creative, inexpensive ideas which appeal to your common sense and helpful nature. What do you do? Do you run the stories? Are you going to permit articles to appear in your magazine that blatantly disparage several of your advertising accounts? If your advertisers say they can prevent wrinkles, are you going to publish articles saying that's not possible? You can't afford to publish negative articles aimed at the financial cornerstones of your business.

That hypothetical fantasy is exactly how many editorial decisions are made. The editor of a major fashion magazine shared with me just such a story. This editor told me about an article she ran that explained how to give an inexpensive dinner party. The suggestion was to decant the expensive liquor bottles and pour in the inexpensive liquor. The result was that many of her major liquor advertisers threatened to cancel their ads for the remaining year. Needless to say, that article and other articles like it never appeared again. And, needless to say, because of this, fashion magazines are not a good source for objective information. That's not to say that the pictures aren't worth a million words, but it takes an objective eye to tell the difference between advertising and fashion updating.

You might think that another good source of information are the cosmetic salespeople at the department stores or in makeup boutiques. I wish they were, but from my research and from the women I've talked to over the years, that isn't usually the case.

Many women have put their faces in the hands of salespeople who often have limited information, experience and training. If they do have training it is the type of sales training I had when I went to work for a department store cosmetic line. They taught me how to improve my selling techniques regardless of whether or not I understood what I was selling or what they were telling me to say.

Before I went about updating this book I intentionally ventured out to the cosmetic counters to see if this product confusion was as rampant as it was when I first started the original project. I found that there was a disconcerting difference: The salespeople were better trained. Not that the salespeople I talked to understood any more about the products they were selling; they just had the *sales talk* down pat.

During several of my *shopping* interviews I got into long discussions trying to pin down exactly what it was they were trying to explain. I asked questions like, "What does *penetrates deeply* mean?" "How deep is *deep*? All the way to my feet?" "What do you mean by protection?" "If nothing can get through can anything get out?" "How does the product do that?" "What ingredient causes that to happen?" "Your cream has the same ingredients as the cream in this line; can it do the same thing?" And on and on . . . Inevitably one of a few things would happen — the salesperson would apologize and say, "That is what we were trained to say and those people must know." Frequently, the salesperson would grab the sales manual and ask me to explain what the more technical descriptions meant. Other salespeople would just brush me off or go get the store manager who would then, in turn, brush me off. The most interesting encounters were with the salespeople who emphatically assured me, regardless of their inability to answer my questions, that their selections for me were wonderful. They steadfastly repeated that the cosmetic line they were selling was the best ever and, if I was even to hope for decent skin, this purchase was vital for my coloring and skin type. Such earnestness always made me wonder if these weren't the top-grossing salespeople around.

If you're like most of the women I've talked to over the years, you've probably more than once bought the entire product line on the belief or chance that this routine would really make a difference. Believing you purchased the basic requirements from someone *in the know*, you took those products home and hoped for the best. Being influenced by the hope of beauty from an expert is very convincing. What occurs more often than not is that one or all of these *wonderful* items caused one of the following things to happen: The products didn't change a thing, they irritated your face or you decided that even though all the products seemed to work, you felt it was all too expensive and too much trouble.

The final source of information we tend to turn to is the category you're reading: the books on the subject of makeup application and skin care. For years I have been reviewing books on the subject of looking good. For the most part, what I have found was a rehash of what the magazines were telling me or, if the explanations did sound different, they were so complicated it was hard to follow. And if it was hard for me to follow, given I was already a makeup artist, I could only imagine what it must be like for other women who are not.

The books that are out there on the market seem to fall into three types of categories. One is the natural approach, which usually deals with skin care. The recipes encourage you to use everything from cucumbers to avocados to mayonnaise; I'll explain later why that is as absurd as it sounds. The second type of books are the ones by the makeup artists to the stars telling me how to apply everyday makeup. In this regard I admit bigotry; I resent these Hollywood artists, who all seem to be men, telling me how easy it is to apply makeup when they don't have to do their own makeup every day. I also include in this category the stars themselves, who, as a result of being famous, now know everything there is to know about looking good. Which they do; they hire someone else to do it for them! The third group of books are either by people who represent makeup lines or are sponsored by the fashion magazines themselves. It always felt to me like I was back again at the beginning with no more answers than when I started.*

Back to the question of who can you trust: Once you finish this book and take a long, objective look at the whole picture, in all its beautiful and beastly aspects, TRUST NO ONE BUT YOUR WELL-INFORMED SELF.

About The Author

Whenever I'm asked by an interviewer to explain my professional credentials I always find that difficult, and that baffles me because autobiographical descriptions are not harder than any other part of writing. They can be more embarrassing, but my nature is not to be modest. I think the problem lies in the details: I'm not sure what to tell you. I'm convinced that you need some amount of information to gauge exactly what kind of expert I am. But do you also want to know about my past? Is it significant to this topic that from the age of 11 (till this very moment) I've been personally dealing with acne to one degree or another or that I went to a dozen or more dermatologists before I decided that they were more of a problem than my acne? What I'm trying to say is that in between all the makeup experience I've had, the rest of my life went on in a particular series of events which seems to have molded and formed why I see and do things the way I do. I would

There are several cosmetic books out on the market that I recommend highly. Please refer to page 251 for a list of those books that will provide good reference material in addition to this one.

like to tell you the in-between parts as well as my professional credentials because that tells the story more accurately. Besides, no matter how much makeup I've done on famous people, that still doesn't tell you a thing about how my makeup philosophies might relate to you.

Two major events that pointed me in this direction of consumer cosmetic specialist were failing miserably at trying to gain a master's degree in neurology from the University of Wisconsin in Madison (although that did give me a science background to understand the technical aspects about makeup), and failing even more abysmally at trying to be an actress (though that gave me the experience of doing makeup for stage and photography). So at the ripe age of 22, with no college degree and no real work skills, I was floundering around, divorced, unemployed and in need of doing something to earn a living.

As fate would have it, I applied for a makeup job at a fashionable makeup boutique in Washington, D.C., and for some unknown reason they hired me. It was true, if I do say so myself, that I had a flair for doing my own makeup, and that is often all the qualification needed to land most makeup sales or artist positions.

A year of experience later (which included my growing clientele of Washington, D.C.'s, notables) the fashionable makeup boutique I was working at started having financial problems and I was laid off. Reluctantly I left that job and went to work for an even more fashionable department store (D.C. had lots of fashionable everything) that carried high-price cosmetic lines. Here I learned firsthand what the world of cosmetic shopping was all about.

I honestly had no idea how sheltered I had been. Up until this time I had bought my makeup piecemeal from places where I could find prices that didn't scare me. The more expensive stuff was completely out of reach. I had no inclination about the dynamics of working in department store cosmetic sales. As it turned out, my indoctrination to this inner sanctum of fashion was short lived: I was fired two weeks after I started. In retrospect I'm surprised they kept me that long.

It was a disaster from the beginning. First, my arrogance (did I mention that I have a tendency to be arrogant?) caused a rift between me and the other saleswomen. I was an artist, not just a salesperson (sure, what special rock did I crawl out from under?). I wanted to sell the colors from all the lines, not just the one I was assigned to. That restriction never made any sense to me; the colors a few feet away were often better for a particular woman than the ones I was supposed to sell. My mistake was spending more time behind the other counters than the one I was assigned to. Second, on more than one occasion I was caught encouraging a customer to use my skin-care routine of 3% hydrogen peroxide and baking soda instead of astringents and scrubs. My selling techniques, from their point of view, were pathetic!

The third and final disaster was the time I argued with one of the Line Representatives in the store about the *healing* properties of a particular product. She told me to sell the cream by saying that it would heal the skin. Before I could do what she asked convincingly and in good faith, I needed to know what was in the cream that performed the function of healing the skin. She pointed out three specifics on the back of the ingredient list. I told her immediately that those ingredients couldn't do what she described. She looked at me in amazement. I picked up another product and said, "Look, here are the exact same ingredients in this one, should I say this one also helps heal the skin?" She sternly informed me that it had to do with the formulation and not the individual ingredients. When I asked what that formulation was, she took the product out of my hand and placed it back on the shelf. "No one needs to know any of that," she insisted and with that walked away before I had the chance to disagree any further. Guess who was asked not to come back the next day?

A few months later my husband received an inviting job offer from The Boeing Company. We packed our bags and headed for what we thought was the Ponderosa, the great Northwest. It wasn't the Ponderosa but there was an openness to ideas that the East Coast didn't share. There also wasn't much competition in the way of professional makeup artists, so I thought it was a logical step to see if I could earn a living on my own, approaching makeup from a practical, nonhype and uncomplicated point of view. There was no one else educating women that contouring the face to make it look different wasn't important, astringents didn't close pores, there weren't wrinkle-free scientists in the Swiss Alps and so-called European skin-care products wouldn't make your face any cleaner than American routines.

By this time after years of fighting acne, I was convinced that my skin care routine (which only cost $10) and what I knew about makeup could help other people. Besides, after getting fired from a traditional makeup job I really had no other choice but to go out on my own. If I went to work for someone else the same thing was going to happen again and again.

In 1981, with a $700 loan from my father (thanks dad), I started a small cosmetic business that sold *no name* makeup straight from the manufacturer. Three years later I had a partner and the business had expanded to four stores. During that time-period I lost 100 pounds (did I mention I used to be fat?) and became single again. I also had a local weekly radio spot, a daily national radio spot, aired a feature report on TV four times a week, was a talk show guest across the country, and finally decided to change careers from makeup to Television Feature Reporter. (In those days I saw myself as a cross between Jane Pauley and Andy Rooney, except I'm not that blonde or short.)

In the spring of 1984 I sold all my shares of the cosmetic business to my partner. The truth is my partner and I had come to a cross-roads. It was a philosophical conflict. She had the financial and management expertise and I was the artistic and publicity expert for the company. Eventually she wanted to know why we weren't selling wrinkle creams or other skin-care products that women seemed to be buying at cosmetic counters everyplace else in the world except in our stores. It got to the point where she didn't understand why we weren't selling blue eyeshadow; if it was so universally popular and easy to sell she felt we should be doing the same. From a business perspective she was right. From my consumer-oriented way of looking at things, I had had enough. Getting out of the makeup business seemed like a breath of fresh air.

At that time I thought I was getting away from makeup and turning in the direction of a television career. I ended up only staying in television for a year. After all those years of working for myself, working for someone else, especially a news director, no matter how glamorous that sounded, felt like a trap. It has turned out to be a good decision. The business I chose instead was publishing and, as you can see, I'm still in the makeup business.

From what I know as a makeup artist mixed with my consumer advocacy position on things, I've continued in the role of the *Ralph Nader of Rouge*. What was true when I first wrote this book remains true. There is no easy way women can gain reliable, realistic information without resorting to technical journals. Without realistic information, women cannot make educated consumer decisions when they buy cosmetics. Even though I'm no longer directly in cosmetics I'm still doing the best I can to counteract the slanted advertisements and biased, misleading information that abounds in fashion magazines and *famous people* beauty books.

Chapter Two

A Cosmetic Quiz — Flights of Advertising Fantasy

Cosmetic Quiz 1

I created the quizzes you'll find scattered through the chapters because I love tests, not all tests, mostly I'm fascinated with the ones you find in fashion magazines. The true and false or yes and no tests that help you discover everything and anything about your likes, dislikes, relationships and feelings. When I see the names of these intriguing, albeit simplistic, tests, headlined on the covers of whatever magazine happens to be sitting in front of me at the doctor's office, I immediately fumble around for a pencil to find out what already seems blatantly obvious. But that never stops me. The only thing that ever stops me is when the doctor announces that it's my turn. In essence, the simplicity of these tests is what makes them so wonderful. They quickly confirm those things my instincts have been telling me all along.

The other reason I created these cosmetic tests is because after all the magazine quizzes I've answered I've never seen one that asks me about makeup or skin care. You would think it would be an easy task, especially for a fashion magazine, to assemble a list of questions that could help women gain insight into how and why they make their cosmetic decisions. It seems to me that these magazine editors are afraid to ask what their readers really think about all those expensively advertised products.

This first test is designed for you to take a good look at your relationship with your makeup. The term "relationship" is actually a good word for describing our attitudes about the cosmetics we buy and wear. Too often it is a one way relationship where we aren't exactly fully participating. We feel either vulnerable or insecure, and the victims of too little or too much information. That sounds like a relationship to me. The question is, how do we get in control of that relationship so we never feel taken advantage of again?

These questions will guide you through your makeup bag giving you the opportunity to examine what you like and don't like about the makeup you're using. They will also help you discover exactly how much you've been *Madison Avenued* into believing the cosmetic industry's advertising campaigns.

The only thing you will need to get started is a pencil. Though if you happen to have a fashion magazine nearby, you can browse through the pages for a few minutes before you answer the following questions:

Examine Your Makeup Attitudes

1. Is there a desire on your part to have your appearance resemble the women in the fashion magazines? **yes no**
2. Do you think makeup can help you achieve that look? **yes no**
3. Do you believe exercise and the right diet can help you achieve that look? **yes   no**
4. Do you feel the right clothes can help you achieve that look? **yes no**
5. Do you feel that no matter what you do, you can't achieve that look? **yes no**
6. If your answer to question 5 is yes, is your answer based on your age? **yes no** Your body type? **yes no** Your financial situation?   **yes no** Your lack of information or knowledge? **yes no**
7. Do you try to get your makeup to look like the models in the magazine? **yes no** Do you think you succeed? **yes no**
8. If the answer to question 7 is no, what do you base your makeup-look on? Personal experimentation? **yes no** Makeup lessons? **yes no**   Hit or miss? **yes no**
9. What area do you have the biggest problems with when

doing your makeup? Foundation? **yes no** Undereye concealer? **yes no**   Blush-on? **yes no** Contour? **yes no**   Lip-lining? **yes no** Lipstick? **yes no** Eyeshadows? **yes no**   Eye-lining? **yes no** Mascara? **yes no** Color selection? **yes no**

10. On a one-to-five scale, five being the most problems and one being the least problems, which cosmetic product(s) do you have the most problem buying? Foundation 1 2 3 4 5 Undereye concealer 1 2 3 4 5 Blush-on 1 2 3 4 5 Contour 1 2 3 4 5 Lipliner 1 2 3 4 5 Lipstick 1 2 3 4 5 Eyeshadows 1 2 3 4 5 Eyeliner 1 2 3 4 5 Mascara 1 2 3 4 5

11. What in particular do you dislike about these products:

	Price	Ease of Blending	Smearing	Lasting	No Problems
Foundation					
Undereye concealer					
Blush-on					
Contour					
Lipliner					
Lipstick					
Eyeshadows					
Eyeliner					
Mascara					

12. Have you purchased a cosmetic that looked different at home than it did in the store? **yes no**
13. Have you purchased a cosmetic that you just didn't like after you started using it? **yes no**
14. Have you purchased an eyeshadow or blush that crumbled when you dropped it, or have you had a blush or eyeshadow compact that you held together with a rubber band regardless of the price? **yes no**
15. Have you purchased a mascara that was labeled water-

soluble and found it difficult to rinse off? **yes no**

16. Have you purchased a mascara that was labeled water-proof and found that it washed right off? **yes no**

17. Do you repeatedly buy lipsticks or glosses that, via the lines around your lips, start making their way to your chin or nose? **yes no**

18a. Have you bought an eyeliner pencil and when trying to sharpen it found that you needed to buy a special sharpener in order to use the pencil? **yes no**

18b. Have you bought the *right* sharpener for your pencil and found that you eventually ended up whittling the pencil down to nearly nothing because the point kept breaking off, smushing away, disappearing or only one side would sharpen while the other retained the wood coating? **yes no**

19. Do you own one-to-five cosmetics that have never been used or used only once? **yes no**

20. Do you own more than one shade of blue eyeshadow? **yes no**

21a. Do you buy most of your makeup from the department store cosmetic counters? **yes no** The drugstore? **yes no** Small boutique or specialty store? **yes no**

21b. If the answer to any part of 21a is yes, if you don't like the product in one line do you feel the next counter or the next cosmetic line will have the answer for you? **yes no**

21c. If the answer to 21b is yes, how many times have you changed lines looking for a solution to your makeup problems? 1 2 3 4 5 6

22. Did you notice that there were almost no models wearing blue eyeshadow or bright lime-green shadow? **yes no**

23. Did you notice a difference between the makeup the models in the ads were wearing and the models in the fashion layouts? **yes no**

24. In general, do you feel misled by the cosmetic industry, either via advertising claims or unreliable, expensive products? **yes no**

And now for the scoring. I originally wanted to eliminate the scoring because I feel the questions and your answers reveal enough all by themselves. But what test is worth taking if there isn't some sort of score card at the end? Even when the breakdowns are totally predictable, I personally love counting up my points and finding a nice, neat category to fit into that helps me see my dilemma explained in black and white. (In the world of cosmetics it's really explanations in multicolored shadows of mauve and terra cotta.) As is true though in any test that reflects opinions and attitudes, regardless of the group you fall into, your own individual feelings are the most important.

Score 2 points for each question you answered yes to and 0 points for each no answer. Total the numbers you circled in question 10. For question 11 count 1 point for each check mark you placed next to a cosmetic you had problems with. Now add up all these points to find your total score.

If you scored between 0 and 30 points, you probably don't wear makeup at all or you only wear lipstick or mascara and even then not all the time. You also probably wash your face with soap and whatever moisturizer you run into. Personally, I think that's great. You haven't wasted one penny at the cosmetic counters. It's true that a little gloss or blush doesn't offer a lot in the way of fashion versatility, but what not wearing makeup lacks in creativity it makes up for in cost-effectiveness. The women who fall into this group often shake their heads at those of us who they think foolishly waste their time and money trying to get all this stuff in the right place. Most of you low-scorers wonder what all the commotion is about in the first place and, to a certain extent, I agree. It's not worth the hassles or the money, though I do happen to think that in terms of being more powerful out in the world of career and fashion it is worth some amount of effort. However, because you took the time to answer these questions, there is something about this subject that has stirred your interest or curiosity. Congratulations for reading this book and protecting yourself before you made too many expensive mistakes.

If you scored between 32 and 64, you are one of the few women who wear makeup without any problems at all. You never waste money because you simply know what you are doing. At this score, your talent is due either to perseverance (you won't stop asking till you grasp exactly how to do it), or you have a natural ability to apply makeup that rivals any professional makeup artist's technique anywhere. It is also possible that you fit into this category because you were born with a fashion-cover look to start with. That means you could apply potash to your skin and still radiate the very definition of fashionable attractiveness. Well, don't worry, I won't hold any of that against you.

A score of 66 to 98 points means you are one of the many who assumes that if you're patient and talk to another expert, you'll find your dream-come-true cosmetic look and be happy. You probably enjoy the hunt-and-search mission of finding a product that works for you. You're challenged by the creation of facial fashion and you're probably fairly handy with your blending technique and color choice. You probably hit on the right items 50% of the time or more. (Though the items are usually not as good as your talent for using them correctly.) Most likely your friends envy your awareness and love playing in your makeup bag. Though, the reason your friends do that is because you frequently give away what you're not using. The down side of all this is the 50% times when you do make poor choices that waste money and time.

A score of 100 to 132 is an interesting group. You've been trying for a long time to figure all this out. You may have had several professional makeup applications done. For the most part you like the way you wear your makeup, but alas, you've given in to the little problems that plague you daily. For example, you probably ignore the smeared eyeliner that winds up under your eye by the end of the day; by now you've learned to *overblend* the foundations that look too pink and the blushers that look like stripes instead of softly colored cheek bones. By now you figure no one notices. You keep secret a personal longing that you would love to create the kind of glamour the fashion magazines portray. I totally understand. You've gotten burned and now you're willing to just let it be. You're not going to stop wearing makeup and you know that your makeup isn't as bad as some and better than others.

This last score, 132 and up, I've divided into two groups. The first group is my favorite. These women are mad as hell and they aren't going to take it anymore; unfortunately they just aren't sure what to take instead. They've tried it all, read it all, seen it all, used it all . . . They've bought all the gift-with-purchases, they've tried the natural and the unnatural route, they've bought the high-end stuff and low-end stuff and now they just want to stuff it. More than the other groups, they bought this book because they think that this anti-industry, pro-makeup book is what they've been looking for all along. I think they may be right.

The second part of the over-132 bunch is a rare breed of consumer. Even though this group scored high they aren't upset. They have both the time and the money to waste. *Any price for beauty* is their motto. If you bought this book, it was in hopes that some of the techniques described in here will work for you (which of course they will), but it had nothing to do with saving money. This group loves the $50.00-an-ounce wrinkle creams or the $15.00 blushes and mascaras. Congratulations, you can afford the eternal search for the perfect makeup product and the cosmetic counters are patiently waiting for your arrival. Possibly the reason you took this test was because it was the only one in the doctor's office while you were waiting for your appointment.

Whether or not you are one of the high scorers and whether or not you can afford to be one or don't want to be, you've bought the right book. We all want to do something about the never-ending quest to deal efficiently and successfully with the person we greet in the mirror every morning and, if I do say so myself, this book is a rational place to begin.

—— Chapter Three ——
The Cinderella Myth

Being Realistic About Cosmetics

I think that sounds easier than it really is. There is not much reality associated with makeup and skin care. Yet, without a firm basis in reality there is no way to approach the cosmetic industry in an objective light. What I mean by reality is keeping your feet on the ground and your head out of the fluff. When it comes to everything from mascara to astringents, expect that they can do nothing earth-shattering for you. There are no cosmetic miracles out there. One company does not have it over any other company. The reality is I haven't found a product that exists within the cosmetic industry that doesn't have a positive AND a negative side to it. There is not a foolproof or fail-safe cosmetic item out there. That doesn't mean there aren't some great things available, but even the great ones have drawbacks. You need to know those things if you're going to keep your feet and face firmly planted in reality.

A good analogy for what I'm talking about would be shopping for a beautiful pair of shoes. The salesperson brings out this absolutely gorgeous to-die-for pair of high heels replete with red Italian leather, studded with multicolored rhinestones that fan out from the pointed toe on back to the elegant 3 1/2-inch heel. They slip on like Cinderella's foot into the glass slipper. As you turn around in the mirror admiring the way they look, your entire profile reflects like something out of a magazine ad. It's amazing what a pair of shoes can do for your appearance. Unfortunately, the storybook never followed Cinderella home after the ball. We were all told that she ran home at 12 midnight because of her fairy godmother's warning. The truth is, dancing in those glass slippers made her feet swell and ache so much she couldn't wait to get home. The dreamy look in her eyes when she was dancing with the prince wasn't because of the prince, it was from thoughts of soaking her aching corns in hot soapy water. And the slipper she left behind wasn't a mistake, she would have gladly left both of them, but she couldn't get the other one off! Get the picture?

Every time I shop for makeup, do my own makeup or do someone else's makeup, I try and remember this image. The before (without makeup) and after (with makeup) differences are indeed dramatic and I would be the last person to deny the power of a beautifully applied makeup. But the first five minutes doesn't relate what it means to keep that look fresh all day long or what it means to get it on in the first place, or what the joy is of finally washing it off at night. The reality of wearing makeup involves some amount of give-and-take along with the expense. Balancing this give-and-take means discovering your best cosmetic options based on the most and LEAST of what you can expect from your makeup. This is the real world of cosmetics I will present to you.

To Correct Or Not To Correct?

The way to start changing the way you look at the ideas promoted by the major cosmetic lines would be to begin with a good working philosophy that you can adopt, to help you form a practical approach to makeup. We've been led to believe that putting on makeup is a process of *correcting* our flaws, minimizing what's wrong with our faces and maximizing what's right! The first premise is based on the assumption that something is wrong with your face and therefore needs makeup to make it right. The second premise is that your strong points aren't strong enough to overcome the bad ones. Great, every morning before you start your makeup and every evening after you wash it off, you're left with your problems hanging out for everyone to see. Unless, of course, you're clever enough to never let yourself be seen without makeup.

Without exception, it is not necessary to apply your makeup with the concept of doing a corrective makeup. The term *corrective makeup* is really an offensive idea. Corrective makeup is a makeup application based on the notion that you should alter the way the face looks by using techniques of shading and contouring. Corrective techniques involve things like changing the shape of the mouth with a lip pencil, shading double chins, highlighting cheekbones, whiting-out smile lines, contouring noses to look less wide or long and placing colors on the eyes that make them appear farther apart. Again, far be it from me to suggest that makeup cannot alter the way the face looks. But the premise that something is wrong and makeup is needed to make it look right is what drives me crazy.

I am frustrated with women going to cosmetic counters or makeup artists and, depending on who they happen to be talking to, being told that there is something wrong with them. Either that their skin is too pink and it should be more yellow, or that their skin is too yellow and should be more pink or that their eyes are too far apart, or too close together, or too small, or too big. And who set those standards anyway? What is the measurement that makes eyes acceptable or lips the *right* size? I do not believe that women are inherently flawed creatures in need of cosmetics to be acceptable.

This probably all sounds strange coming from someone who wears a good deal of makeup. But remember, I'm not challenging the wearing of makeup, I'm challenging our attitudes and egos when it comes to how we feel about it. There are so many creative options available that getting caught up in a corrective makeup application is a waste of energy.

I know this may sound corny but it truly helps to believe that with or without your makeup on, your face is fine. Yes, even without mascara, there is nothing that needs changing or altering about your face. I know this is a hard idea to swallow, especially if you've been well-indoctrinated into the world of fashion or a well-established social life, but the truth is, the world won't stop and you won't be unloved without your makeup on. **THAT DOESN'T MEAN I'M ADVOCATING NOT WEARING MAKEUP**. What I am talking about is freedom so that you don't have to be a victim addicted to your foundation and blusher.

This subject of being okay the way you are reminds me of the time I was meeting a woman friend for a casual breakfast in a neighborhood restaurant. The best we both could accomplish that morning was brushing our teeth and slipping on a pair of warmups. As we greeted each other at the table we both commented on how relaxed we felt and thanked the powers that be for Sunday mornings. The conversation continued like this: My friend mentioned how good I looked without makeup on. I teased her by saying she needn't sound so surprised and we laughed. I then said she looked great too. She insisted that she looked terrible without makeup on and I was only returning her compliment to be polite. After a few exchanges of, "No I really mean that," and, "How could you say that I look awful," I quickly responded by saying, "Look, this is what I do for a living! I never tease about the way someone looks, just like I would never expect you to tease me about my car or life insurance" (my friend happened to be my insurance agent). "And second, why do you assume I look good without makeup on and you don't? Have you considered this might be an emotional response on your part based on a lack of self-acceptance? Or, for the sake of argument, let's say I agree with you; you do look worse without your makeup on. What do you do now? If someone is attracted to you for your makeup instead of you for who you are as a wonderful, dear, kind, adorable human being, are you going to live in your makeup bag? If someone likes you for your makeup, give it to them. If that's what they want, they should have it."

After our lengthy discussion, we agreed that most women feel the way she does. They argue in a most frighteningly convincing manner over how terrible they look without their makeup on or how much weight they haven't lost or how terrible their hair is. When it comes to makeup, this insecurity has made them choose to live their lives behind a mask instead of in a world of options that can be creative, exciting and spontaneous. Makeup can be a fashion complement to any woman's features and, like fashion, makeup is an alternative, not a necessity. The same way you wear jeans versus a dress depending on the occasion or your mood, choosing to wear a little, a lot, or no makeup at all is the same process. Any other attitude is limiting and at the same time encourages a lack of self-worth and -esteem.

The path to a simple and attractive application is to define and color each feature as it exists without thinking that you're changing anything. Whether it be casual, dramatic, business-oriented, glamorous, natural, daring, sophisticated, preppy or whatever, it still can involve the same basic techniques. (For example, regardless of the style of blouse, there are only so many ways to button it.) The idea that corrective makeup application is an everyday application strategy is unnecessary. Now, doesn't that sound easier already?

Beauty Is A Dated Word

So what is lurking at the bottom of all those makeup items we've been talking about with such heartfelt skepticism? **Power**. Yes, I said power. If we could change the belief that makeup makes us beautiful and accept that what it's really doing is making us more powerful, we'd deal with the whole subject more clearly. The term beauty even sounds antiquated. It conjures up images of the 1950s, where getting ready was something we did for hours as a way to land a husband or be more popular. We were so sweet back then when we needed to excuse ourselves to powder our respective noses or fix our lipstick. How we reveled when our heartbroken tears would cause our chivalrous dates to dab away the black streams of mascara cascading down our cheeks, reassuring us that everything was going to be okay. Well, gag me with a spoon. May the '50s rest in peace and stay there.

That was then as this is now so let me try a more current example to make my point. As long as we are on the subject of dates, let me tell you what a man I was going out with once told me. We had been seeing each other for a few months, and it just happened that whenever we got together it was usually after work or before some special evening event. Those are the two times I almost always makeup. That meant he had never seen me without my professional look in place. Then one afternoon we got together to do something more casual, which is a time I always take advantage of for not wearing any makeup or for wearing only mascara and a little lipstick. He commented several times about how nice I looked. At one point he said very sincerely that he preferred me without all *that stuff* on my face. I asked him what was wrong with the way I did my makeup? "What was I with makeup on, chopped liver?" He insisted nothing was wrong with the way I did my makeup, he said I just looked good without it. His rationale was, if it didn't make me look any better, why did I bother?

I knew he felt he was giving me a compliment by telling me I was more attractive naturally. He took for granted that all women wear makeup because it makes them look better and if they looked fine without it they would stop wearing it. He's probably right. Most women do wear makeup because they think it makes them look better. We've been taught very carefully to feel that way. But why take that self-deprecating attitude if it isn't the truth? Makeup may make you feel better, but that's an emotional response. It may also make you look more fashionable, but that's a societal attitude. You can feel attractive or unattractive anytime you want; it's up to you, not your makeup. You may blame it on your makeup, but it's still you and the way you feel.

I wear makeup because it is a useful tool for me when I need it. It can be powerful as well as helpful. It adds a flair to my presence and people like seeing that. Now, that's powerful. But it isn't always powerful. Sometimes makeup gets in the way. A full makeup with a bathing suit looks weird, not beautiful. Or if you're looking to be intimate with a significant other, it can get in the way. Think about it. After spending time neatly applying your makeup, how eagerly are you going to want to kiss or hug anyone, much less a man you're intimate with? Unless of course he doesn't mind walking around with half your face on his collar. And what can you say when that happens? "Excuse me, when I hugged you just now, I left part of my cheek on your shirt sleeve." Doesn't that sound intimate?

Now, I know there's a reality to the idea that makeup makes pale, tired skin appear more alive — but why adopt that attitude when it creates such a negative self-image and self-imposed trap? Using makeup as a way to be more versatile, more fashionable or more powerful is definitely a more liberating attitude than the notion of: "With makeup on I'm more beautiful." When it comes to wearing makeup, always do what is best for you at any given time, being aware of how makeup can work for you, or against you.

Being Realistic About Yourself

I know this next statement isn't going to shock you, but beauty is far from skin deep. I'm not talking esoterically, I'm referring to the fact that all the makeup in the world done by the most talented makeup artists won't change 25 pounds of excess weight, the smell of cigarette smoke and overly permed hair with 1/2-inch roots that are screaming for someone to color them. Catch my drift?

Being attractive is a way of existing in the world that exudes health, energy and love for life. Did that just sound like a milk commercial or what? But it is what I mean. Away from the soft focus of TV lights, the best makeup in the world won't hide exhaustion, bad health and unhappiness. This book isn't meant to deal with any of those issues, but they are something to think about as you consider what it is you want to project to the world and what you can expect to create with your makeup. Getting your total appearance together is part of the entire package called you.*

Speaking of soft focus, it's no surprise to anyone that magazines and television create an illusionary world that can be misleading. A lipstick all by itself will not make you look like a model. As you've noticed by now, advertising campaigns often use pubescent models that happen to be annoyingly perfect. These ads suggest that their products can make you look just like these adolescents. Actually, we don't fall for that ploy quite like we used to and there are *somewhat* older well-known models around, but for the most part it is the young ones that do the ads.

Facts are facts, and neither childhood nor genetically in-herited good skin can be bottled. No matter how hard we wish for it, there is no fountain of youth lurking at the bottom of makeup products. Though, it is important to note that a well-applied makeup and an effective skin-care routine can indeed make you look wonderful. But that is a different issue from expecting cosmetic products to heal, cure or change every skin problem and insecurity you may happen to have.

Brand-Name Addiction

Together with my feelings about corrective makeup and makeup addiction, it is my strong belief that product loyalty does not make any sense. The success of the major product lines in establishing that loyalty becomes apparent in how a woman responds to the question about what brand of makeup she is presently using. The answer usually reflects the amount of money she has spent on said product. A customer usually

There are several books on the subject of health and appearance that I highly recommend. Please refer to page 251 for the suggested reading list.

whispers when she is using a bargain brand, and if she's using the expensive brand you can hear her across the room. The reality is that the cost of any cosmetic product has nothing to do with whether it will work for you or not. I have used both inexpensive and expensive makeup which looked wonderful and was good for the skin, as well as expensive and inexpensive makeup that looked awful.

Advertising executives would like us to believe that when we give our loyalties and money to their cosmetic line, their company is manufacturing the makeup for us. That isn't necessarily the case. What is really happening?

Pretend you buy a brand-name eyeshadow from two different companies. Did you know that these two eyeshadows could be absolutely the same eyeshadow? I mean exactly the same eyeshadow? How? Simple. Both companies purchased it from the same manufacturer. What they do to the cosmetic after they purchase it is also relatively the same. They package it, distribute it, promote it and sell it. So you, the consumer, might pay anywhere from $3.00 to $12.00 for the exact same eyeshadow, depending on whose name is on the package, or compact.

Shortly after I opened my first makeup store I had the opportunity to visit one of the manufacturing plants that was wholesaling their makeup to me. As they proudly toured me around their facilities showing me the rows and rows of material and machinery, we passed an area where they were assembling eyeshadow tins. At the end of this conveyor were boxes labeled with most of the major cosmetic brand names. They obviously wanted me to know that I would be selling the same stuff these big shots were selling. They were right, I was impressed. I was also pleased to know firsthand how things really happened.

What I have just described is the reality of the cosmetic industry. I'm hardly the first person to discover this. The television show *60 Minutes* did a segment on this very issue, and

Ralph Nader has argued the point himself on numerous talk shows and in his own book on the cosmetic business.

The long and short of it is that no matter who's making your makeup, the end results are that you could get stuck with a 500% on up to 2000% increase in what you pay for the final product if you buy according to packaging or advertising claims rather than effect. The package doesn't tell you who made the product and the price doesn't reflect anything about the quality, how it will go on the skin, or how long the effect you're looking for will last. When women ask me what I think about a particular brand of cosmetics, my response, regardless of the line, is always the same: **THE BRAND NAME DOESN'T MATTER.** There are products in all the lines that are wonderful, mediocre, awful or just a total waste of money. The only way to ascertain that is to try the stuff on and see what happens.

Why is it then that a particular brand of cosmetic gets to be so expensive, compared to a less expensive brand that has been purchased from the same manufacturing company? In the final analysis, price is determined by what the market will bear. If you're willing to pay $25.00 for a foundation and believe you'll look $25.00 better, they'll sell it to you for just that. Hopefully, by now your ideas of brand-name loyalties have changed. Don't take my word for it! Go to any library and check out a copy of *Drug and Cosmetic Industry* magazine and you can read about the manufacturing of cosmetics and cosmetic ingredients. This periodical will reveal how the cosmetic industry works. It will also announce how cosmetic chemists and executives are always leaving one company to go and work for another, so the idea of cosmetic secrets existing isn't really possible.

Think about it this way: It doesn't matter whose name is on the package, what the ads say or how expensive it is; if the makeup works and feels good on your skin, use it. That's not a difficult concept and it's what we're really talking about once we throw out the boxes, close the magazines and put the cosmetics on. You must be aware of all of these factors in the buying and use of cosmetics in today's high-pressure, sales-oriented environment.

A New Wrinkle In Skin-Care Promises

April 1988 News Flash: The Federal Drug Administration, which many of us thought had been ridiculously lax in allowing the cosmetic industry to repeatedly make absurd and reckless claims about products, has hopefully changed its head-turning ways. The FDA is taking action against several cosmetic companies, telling them to tone down their *trip to Jupiter* claims or face the risk of injunctions or seizure of their merchandise.

Drugs are defined as those things that change the structure or function of the body, cosmetics are those things that improve the appearance of skin or cover up that appearance. Improving the appearance or covering up the appearance are acceptable claims. Cosmetic ads that use words like repairing, restructuring or otherwise altering the skin are no longer acceptable. Does this mean the consumer will notice a difference in cosmetic advertising? Probably not. I'm sure what will happen instead is that the ad execs will utilize more carefully constructed slogans that contain words which indicate the same feeling as before without crossing the FDA's special dictionary guidelines. Now that's what I call a *microscopically penetrating* sign of change that no one will likely ever be able to see.

Advertising: Fact Or Fiction?

This is about the time you might be asking about truth in advertising. It is without question one of my favorite questions because I often ask myself the same question. How can they say what they say and not get in trouble? The Federal Trade Commission is the watchdog here, and the cosmetic industry has cute ways of getting around the details of its guidelines. Cosmetic advertising is a prime example of the deceptive, manipulative use of the English language. It conveys an impression without substantiating anything at all. When you can't truthfully say a product will do something, you say that it can help to do something or will affect something which sounds beneficial. The claims go on and on. I've listed some of my favorites with an explanation of the what-they-aren't-telling-you:

"Realistic help is here."

Well, what's realistic to you and what's realistic for the product is subjective. They don't list out what they specifically mean by the word *realistic*. Realistic could mean no help at all. The same applies to the word *help*. What I think is help and what they mean by help can be two entirely different things.

"Works with the microcirculation of your skin."

Works with is always a good phrase: Exactly what kind of *work* is it referring to? *Microcirculation* sounds very impressive. Yet microcirculation is only the tiny capillaries near the surface of the skin. If I take my finger and touch the surface of my face, I will automatically affect the microcirculation of my skin. If I take a cream and rub it into the skin, I affect the microcirculation the same way. The cream isn't necessarily doing anything — just your hand.

"Penetrates deeply into the layers of the skin."

Penetrates is one of the most misleading terms the cosmetic industry uses. Everything, if it is a small enough molecule, will penetrate into the skin. Most moisturizers have too large a molecular structure to penetrate entirely into the skin. When a moisturizer *can* penetrate into the skin, the word *layers* becomes misleading. One layer of skin is so microscopically small as to be beyond human description. The cream can penetrate thousands of layers and still not have traveled anywhere. And even if the cream could penetrate deep into the skin it would be absorbed and flushed out, which is what you would want it to do. You wouldn't want the skin to try and use the preservatives, fragrance and coloring agents as well as the so-called beneficial ingredients. The entire concept assumes you can change the skin from the outside-in by absorbing some benefit from the cream, and that is not possible from a cosmetic. If it were possible the cosmetic would no longer be a cosmetic: It would become a drug and fall under different FDA (Federal Drug Administration) guidelines.

"Look younger, too."

This is my favorite. Well, how much younger? Ten years or ten minutes? The word *younger* is so vague, it could mean ten seconds. The word *too* implies that you can look as young as the women in their ads are claiming to look as a result of using their product. Do you really believe that their models look young because of this moisturizer? They look young because they are young.

"Replaces the fluids of youth."

Human beings are mostly water, which includes babies, children and adults. If I put some water in the product I'm selling and add oil and wax (which are the main ingredients in ALL moisturizers), the water and the oils stay on the skin for a while and then zap, I've replaced your basic *fluids of youth*.

"The skin's ability for self-rejuvenation is helped."

I've never been quite sure what they mean by self-rejuvenation. It sounds to me like a fancier way to say "look younger, too." Rejuvenate means to restore youth. The same question applies here as before, how much youth is restored? A few minutes? A few hours? One week? Then again, it suggests that it's the skin's natural ability to rejuvenate itself, is being aided. I wonder what process they're referring to.

"Medically tested"

You're never shown the test results nor is the lab or chemist mentioned. It can also be reworded to read *scientifically formulated*, or *laboratory-tested*, which sounds very scientific. Well, what product isn't scientifically formulated or somehow created in a lab setting?

"Natural"

Natural is one of those great marketing terms that automatically sounds like what you're buying must be good for you. Natural conjures up images of health and safety; safe to use and healthy for the skin. Vitamins, herbs and anything that doesn't sound like a chemical falls into this imaginary natural sphere. Imaginary because natural has nothing intrinsically to do with health or herbs. The confusion is that natural and good, natural and healthy, and natural and safe are not the same thing. I can think of many things that are natural which are anything but healthy or safe for the skin: ammonia, sulphuric acid, urine, formaldehyde, glass, rock, and so on.

If buying a natural product made you feel that you were getting something that didn't contain all those nasty *chemicals*, think again. Whether or not it is labeled natural does not tell you a thing about what you are buying. There are no guidelines surrounding what can or cannot be inside a natural product. Cosmetics called natural still contain preservatives, coloring agents and all the other things you can think of that sound very unnatural.

"Hypoallergenic"

Hypoallergenic is one of the greatest nonsense words I've ever heard. According to the dictionary, hypoallergenic means less than allergenic. It ostensibly indicates that the product should be less than likely to cause an allergic reaction. That would be great if that were possible, but it isn't even potentially possible. First, there are no guidelines to regulate what can be used in a so-called hypoallergenic product. Second, in 1978 the United States District Court of Appeals disallowed the term hypoallergenic as having any legal meaning. And third, there is no way a product, regardless of what it is called, can know what you, as an individual, will be allergic to. What makes me scratch and sneeze may be different from what makes you blotch and turn red. There is no way a hypoallergenic product can be less allergic for everybody. Knowing what will cause you to react is a hit-and-miss process of discovering what ingredients are problematic for you, and you alone.

"Deep cleansing"

This term has always baffled me. How deep is *deep*? Sounds like a dentist cleaning your teeth. I can vividly hear the sound of the drill trying to get into the skin. If a product could clean deeply, I mean really *deeply*, it would mean you'd be bleeding. On the other hand, if they figuratively meant "deep clean" to represent a thorough cleansing, that would be fine. But most women believe that somehow these deep-cleansing products can somehow get into a pore and remove a blackhead from the inside out. There isn't a product anywhere that can accomplish that. If there were such a product I would have found it and you would have too and neither of us would ever have a problem with blackheads again. No matter how many products I have bought that claimed they could clean out pores, dry up oil and remove blackheads, they have never once accomplished what they said they could do.

"Gentle to the skin"

Products that call themselves *gentle to the skin* often cannot substantiate that claim by their ingredients. But that doesn't stop them from slapping that claim on their label. Much like hypoallergenic, there are no guidelines or specifications about what constitutes a gentle product. If you don't read the ingredient listing you won't know that you're buying something that isn't gentle until you put it on your face (and then it's too late).

Chapter Four

Skin Care — And Now For Something That Is Still Completely Different

Quiz 2

We are about to broach the subject of cleansing your face. The following questions give you the chance to evaluate your knowledge and feelings about your skin and cleansing routine. I am hoping that they will start a pathway to some clearer and more logical decision-making. It seems apparent from the various types of creams, cleansers and masks women buy that most of those choices are based on advertising whimsy and little else.

There is a tendency in cosmetic ads and from cosmetic experts to do one of two things: give too much information that you couldn't possibly understand without a master's degree in chemical engineering or give no objective information at all. The latter, no information, is the hardest for me to deal with: You've seen those ads that show beautiful models tossing their hair and bodies around bragging about how good they look as a result of a particular product. Then comes the punch line: They don't know what's in this fantastic cosmetic, they don't care what's in it and, of course, all you should care about is that it works, for them. Great logic. Then for sure the cosmetic companies don't have to disclose any intelligent information. If their models don't care, why should you?

Most of the questions I've been asked about skin problems could be easily answered if there wasn't confusion regarding the basic facts about what skin and skin-care products can and cannot do. But before I get too much more ahead of myself, find a pencil and fill in the quiz that follows:

Face Facts — Skin-Care Quiz

1. Do you know what type of skin you have? **yes no**
2. Has your skin type changed in the past five years?
   yes no
3. Does your skin type change during the year? **yes no**
4. If the answer to question 3 was yes, does your skin change with the seasons? **yes no**   With your stress level? **yes no** With your menstrual cycle? **yes no**
5. Do you change your skin-care routine when your skin type changes? **yes no**
6. If the answer to question 3 was yes, when your skin changes do you buy new products to take care of it?
   yes sometimes no
7. Do you tend to purchase those products from the same line you've been using? **yes no**
8. Do you believe that it is best to use together only products from the same line? **yes sometimes no**
9. Do you feel you have sensitive skin?
   yes sometimes no
10. Do you sleep in your makeup? **yes sometimes no**
11. If the answer to question 10 was yes, do you tend to have problems the next morning with swollen eyes or breakouts? **yes sometimes no**
12. If you have *normal* skin, do you feel that is a result of your skin-care routine? **yes no**
13. Do you read the ingredient labels on the products you are considering purchasing for your skin?
    yes sometimes no
14. Are you impressed by long lists of ingredients? **yes no**
15. Do you comparison-shop the different skin-care lines that are available? **yes sometimes no**
16. Do you base your skin-care selections on the information you've read in a magazine? **yes sometimes no** You've been given by a friend? **yes sometimes no** You've received from the salesperson?
    yes sometimes no
17. Do you assume dry skin ages more than oily skin? **yes no**

18. Do you believe that there are cosmetic moisturizers available that can change the wrinkles you already have?
yes no

19. Do you believe that there are cosmetic moisturizers available that can prevent or inhibit wrinkling? **yes no**

20. If you are presently using an astringent or toner, why do you use one? To close pores? **yes no** To freshen the skin after your cleanser? **yes no** To remove the last traces of makeup or debris from the skin? **yes no** Because it's part of the routine you were told to follow?
yes no

21. How many different types of astringents have you purchased over the past five years? 1 2 3 4 5

22. How many different types of moisturizers have you purchased over the past five years? 1 2 3 4 5

23. How many different cosmetic skin-care lines have you tried over the past five years? 1 2 3 4 5

24. After you clean your face, before you use your astringent or moisturizer, how does your skin feel? Dry? **yes no**
Oily? **yes no** Normal? **yes no**

25. When the salesperson explains how a cleansing product works, do you understand what she is explaining? **yes sometimes no**

26. Do you know what collagen in a cosmetic product does for the skin? If yes, circle one or more of the following: Plumps the skin **yes no** Retains moisture **yes no** Prevents wrinkles **yes no**

27. Do you use a different moisturizer around your eyes than on the rest of your face? **yes sometimes no**

28. If the answer to question 27 was yes, why do you use a different moisturizer around your eyes than on your face? Circle one or more of the following that applies: The skin around the eyes is different from the rest of the face so it needs a different moisturizer. **yes no** The moisturizers are formulated differently. **yes no** The salesperson said it would be better for my skin. **yes no** I want to prevent lines around my eyes. **yes no**

29. Have you ever seen a dermatologist for acne? **yes no**

30. Have you had success with the routine your dermatologist prescribed for you? **yes no**

31. If the answer to question 30 was no, why not? Skin still broke out. **yes no** Skin irritation got worse. **yes no** Too expensive? **yes no** The doctor told me not to wear makeup and I wasn't willing to do that. **yes no**

32. Do you have facials on a regular or semi-regular basis? **yes no**

33. Do you regularly use a sunscreen? **yes no**

34. Do you feel radiation from tanning machines is safe for the skin? **yes no**

35. Do you feel there is a difference between sun-damaged wrinkles and genetically inherited wrinkles? **yes no**

36. Are you curious to learn more about Retin-A? **yes no**

Congratulations, you've made it through one more quiz. To find your score, count 5 points for each question you answered yes to, 3 points for sometimes and 0 points for no. Then add up the numbers you circled for questions 21, 22 and 23. The sum of these totals is your score.

If you scored between 0 and 40 points, you probably only wash your face with soap and water and even then not all the time. If that's true for you, it's due to one of two reasons; either your skin is perfect, or regardless of what your skin does, you feel, why bother? If the former description is the case, you're the type who wouldn't recognize a pimple if your life depended on it. If you saw an open pore you would probably fall into it by mistake. Peaches-and-cream complexion is a euphemism women curse at you under their breath. For all intents and purposes, you're not worried about wrinkles because you don't really have any wrinkles yet and most of the older women in your family don't have any either, so you figure the odds are in your favor. And besides all that, you're probably consistent about using a sunscreen. You also haven't wasted any money on skin care, at least not yet. (If this description fits you, you are allowed to read this book anyway.)

If the second description fits — regardless of what your skin does, you don't bother — this is more troublesome. It is the opposite scenario from someone who is a high scorer. The difference is that the high scorer spends money in hopes of changing her situation but can't find the right solution. You have skin problems but don't want to go through the muck and mire of products and a maze of boring, unimportant information to find out what works. I understand your reluctance totally. If that is the case for you and you are resistant to reading through the entire skin-care chapter, before bailing out, just jump to page 140 and try the routine without the explanation. Don't misunderstand, I'm not advocating that as your best option; but it's better than giving up at this point.

If you scored between 40 and 80, you're either very young (under the age of 24) and haven't been shopping long enough to accumulate that many points, or you have pretty good skin and buy skin-care products that you feel are easy and worth the price. You've chosen a simple routine of three products and you're satisfied with those. The only possible hitch is that you're beginning to be concerned that with each passing year you might have to start doing more and that makes you nervous (which is why you bought this book). I agree, it makes me nervous too, so read this chapter thoroughly before spending a penny on any potential *age paranoia* you may be secretly harboring.

A score of 80 to 110 is my kind of group. These women love being good to themselves without going foolishly overboard. They don't consider themselves taken advantage of at the makeup counters because they never get talked into buying everything. In general they never overbuy, they buy only what they need. These women love the feel of a new moisturizer gliding over their skin, but they buy a new one only when the one at home is empty. They also love the occasional splurge of seeing a facialist. If this group has used more than one cosmetic line, they've changed not so much out of frustration as out of the fun of trying something different. They don't really waste money because they use the products they buy. But they also don't realize how much they could save.

This last score, 110 and up, was me 10 years ago. I had acne and I would try anything to get rid of it. Every mirror I passed was a constant reminder of the embarrassment I felt with every lump or white surface that reared its ugly little head. Dermatologists, skin-care products, toners, specialty bar soaps, cover-up creams, drying lotions, facials . . . If it was out there I would find it. Of course nothing ever changed, but I kept on trying.

Not every woman who falls in this group is compelled by acne to constantly try different products and treatments. This group also includes women who simply are not satisfied with their skin or the products they use. In all fairness, this discontent is not always due to the routine itself. Some of these women will never be pleased with their skin, particularly their wrinkles. But even a miscellaneous blackhead or pimple can send them to a new dermatologist or a new skin-care line. Whatever it is, they desperately want to change it and this desperation keeps their hopes up. Then, as soon as they hear about something that sounds new, especially from a friend who swears by it, they're willing to give it a try. It becomes a vicious cycle with no end in sight, except maybe until now.

Skin Care From The Outside In

As I look over the material and research I've accumulated, it seems amazing to me how involved it all is. You wouldn't think that cleaning the face could be so complicated or shrouded in such controversy, but it is. Perhaps the explanation for this is that the face, even though it occupies such a small surface area of the body, manifests a lot of topical problems: acne, wrinkles, sagging skin, sunburns, blackheads, dryness, irritation, eczema and allergies, not to mention our very notions of what beauty is all about. No wonder it's so complicated and hard to sort through.

Before I do any of that let me mention something concerning the skin-care regimen you are presently using: **IF IT WORKS FOR YOU, IF YOU ARE SATISFIED WITH HOW YOUR SKIN LOOKS AND FEELS, CONTINUE DOING EXACTLY WHAT YOU ARE DOING.** If you feel you aren't spending too much money and all the products make your skin happy, there is absolutely no reason in the world to change. I don't want anyone to use a new routine, mine or anyone else's, unless they're dissatisfied with what they're presently doing!

My ideas and suggestions are an option and an alternative to many of the things you are probably already using. There is no reason to change just for the sake of change. Statistics indicate that most women who buy cosmetics change their cleansing routine every three-to-five years. The odds are you will eventually be one of those who changes their skin-care routine and tries something new. When you're ready, what you are about to read could change the way you spend money on skin care forever. Without question it has to be one of the easiest and most inexpensive routines there is. When you're ready these ideas will still be a valid way to take care of your skin. I've followed my own advice for almost 10 years now.

Forget Skin Type?!

You knew that the first question of the quiz was a trick question didn't you? After all, I've been promising to shake up your long-standing beliefs so why not start from the beginning with *skin type*? Knowing your skin type has been a cornerstone of the cosmetic industry for a long time. In my opinion it is one of the most creative marketing plans around: Develop a need and create products that will supposedly handle that need. It has become so sophisticated that some companies use computers to help you find what should already be evident by looking in the mirror. That's not to say that some understanding of skin type isn't important; it's just not the way the cosmetic industry approaches it.

The cosmetic industry's approach to skin type focuses on solving a problem with products designed for your particular situation. This notion revolves around the media-constructed concept of what normal skin is supposed to be. Then, if your skin type is something other than normal, their products suggest they can bring it back to the status quo of normal.

The very idea of normal skin as being an attainable goal is unrealistic for many reasons. First it ignores the dynamics and ever-changing status of our skin. Even women with perfect complexions will go through phases of having oily or dry skin. They may even have breakouts once in a while. Given that skin is so volatile, no one is likely to have normal skin for very long no matter what they do.

Second, skin type suggests that once you are *typed* your skin stays that way, at least for a while, and that isn't true either. Day to day, month to month and season to season the face is subject to emotions, weather conditions, menstrual cycles and whatever else life brings with it. All those things can directly affect skin type in a hundred different ways. If your skin-care routine focuses on type, then your routine becomes obsolete the moment the season changes, or you decide to change boyfriends. What do you do then, run out and buy new products?

The third problem is the way skin type is determined. If I was to ask what is your skin type, you could only answer it based on what your skin feels like today. If I then make a decision on what products you should use based on the information you've just told me, we would both be making a big mistake. The skin type your face feels like right now is primarily a result of the way you clean your face. That routine can be creating the problems you're seeing. In other words, if you wash every day with a bar soap (which is drying) and then follow up with a moisturizer (which can be greasy and potentially block pores), that can create a severe combination skin condition. Or, if you wipe off your makeup with creams (which are greasy) then follow up with a toner (which is drying) you should not be surprised at all if you develop a combination skin condition accompanied by dry patches and breakouts. Typing skin without taking into consideration what is presently being used assumes that the skin is the way it is all by itself, regardless of what you do to it and that is not true. Before we can know what our skin is or is not, sometimes we have to start back at square one before we can go forward.

The last reason why skin type can be misleading is, because what happens when all the skin types are present? For me, I've recently developed dry skin patches, I still breakout, lines are starting to show up, and I have very oily skin. Interesting isn't it? If I followed what they told me at the cosmetic counters I would have to buy a little bit of everything to handle all those problems. And that is not an unusual problem for women, to have a little bit of each skin type going on simultaneously, or overlapping each other.

Having explained all of that, it is now safe to list the ever-popular, ever-misleading skin-type categories. I know it may seem hypocritical to include a list I find so unreliable, but without a consistent understanding of what those traditional terms mean it will be harder to determine where you are, at any given time. Especially if you're new at the skin-care game. The purpose of this list is to make sure that when I talk about dry, oily, sensitive or normal skin, you will know exactly what I'm describing. But **DO NOT** use these individual categories as the way to determine your skin-care routine. For the time being use this list as a dictionary of terms and nothing else.

The following list is a combination of industry standard definitions for skin type and my opinions. The parentheses indicate where I disagree with certain parts of the standard definition for that skin type.

Normal skin: No visible pores, no dry skin, few lines (as if having lines is not normal), few to no breakouts and no excess oil to speak of.

Oily skin: Visible pores and blackheads, small breakouts mostly occurring around the nose, cheeks and chin. Few lines (as if oily skin doesn't age) and a lot of excess oil that gets worse as the day goes by.

Dry skin: No visible pores, skin tends to flake and peel, dry patches, cracked dry lips and as the day goes by the skin feels more dry and tight. You also feel that you have more lines than you should at your age (who feels they have less lines than they should?).

Sensitive skin: (This one is my definition.) Regardless of the presence of any other skin type, your skin tends to react to everything and the evidence of that reaction shows up immediately on the surface of the face. (See the next chapter for further details.)

Mature skin: Skin tends to have its share of wrinkles, and dry, flaky skin is almost always present. Oily skin is rarely a problem though large pores may be evident if the skin has spent many years baking in the sun. Some amount of sagging around the jowl and jaw line is noticeable and the eyes mirror the same wear and tear.

SUMMARY: Skin type does exist, but it is created in conjunction with your skin-care routine, the weather, your diet, emotions and makeup routine. We are also not exclusively one category or the other. Frequently more than one skin condition can be present at the same time. The advertising gimmick of normal skin is a frustrating myth that is more like the proverbial carrot in front of the horse: always there never to be reached. Because of that passionate search to achieve perfect skin we end up doing and spending too much for too little return.

But Don't Forget Sensitive Skin

You really can't avoid sensitive skin. Like the definition in the preceding section — regardless of your primary skin type a myriad of minor irritating skin conditions can be present. The skin can burn, chafe, crack and have patchy areas of dry, flaky skin. It can also breakout in small diaper-rash-looking bumps, itch, swell, blotch, and easily redden, and is likely to develop allergic reactions to cosmetics, animals, dust and pollen. Most of us have sensitive skin to one degree or another because skin is an extremely sensitive body organ.

The idea that most of us have sensitive skin isn't such an unreasonable supposition. The skin is hanging out there in the midst of all the things that the rest of the body doesn't want. Your skin is the protective armor to keep the elements and everything else imaginable from penetrating through and invading your insides. The only way we can protect the skin is with clothing, and because we tend to wear clothes over most of our anatomy except the face, that leaves our faces painfully exposed to everything. Therefore sensitive skin is probably the most normal type of skin to have.

Most skin-care routines separate what they recommend for women with sensitive skin types, from what they recommend for other skin types. One of the reasons I wanted you to forget skin type is because I treat everybody as having the potential for all the skin types. The same precautions in essence exist for each and that means treating the skin gently. Whether or not you think of your face as being sensitive, oily, dry or mature, you still need to be gentle with your skin.

The operative word for the rest of this book is **GENTLE**. The do's and don'ts list is almost the same for all skin types. Where differences exist they will be boldly pointed out. But for the most part if it's bad for sensitive skin it is probably bad for oily skins, dry skins and mature skin. As this information on gentle skin treatment unfolds it will slowly solve a lot of skin mysteries.

Finally, Let's Clean The Face

Before you can begin any makeup routine you always start with taking the makeup off instead of putting on. This is hardly a new thought, but it bears repeating: Makeup always needs to go on over a clean face. No wonder skin care is 70% of the cosmetic business. You can't get started without it.

The cleansing routine I recommend starts with water. THE MOST IMPORTANT PART OF CLEANING YOUR FACE IS USING WATER. That's right, good old-fashioned H_2O. Not water by itself, of course, but I'll soon explain what you use with the water. Let me explain the four reasons why water is so important:

1. Water is abundant. As a natural resource it is 75% of our environment, which makes water the most inexpensive item you can use on your face.

2. Water is an integral part of the human system. Human beings are about 70% water, which makes water compatible to everyone's skin. Wait, I take that back. I've learned over the years never to say never, and never to say everyone. I'm sure there is someone out there somewhere who is indeed allergic to water, though the chances of that being true for you are at best remote.

3. Water is GENTLE. But water is not automatically gentle. Water is only gentle when it is tepid. Hot water burns the skin and cold water will shock it. If the goal is to be gentle (and it is) then tepid water is essential.

4. Water is frictionless. When you splash your face with water your hands glide over the face preventing you from pulling at the skin. That means you can remove your makeup without tugging at your face. This can prevent irritation and reduce some amount of premature aging. Constantly wiping, tugging and pulling on the skin stretches out some of the skin's inherent elasticity. Like a rubber band it can only take so much pulling till it won't snap back anymore.

As essential as water is to any cleansing routine, water alone is not enough. Water by itself will not remove the oil from the skin or all of your makeup. Even when the makeup is predominantly water soluble, it is rarely 100% water soluble, especially when combined with your own natural oil, or your favorite moisturizer. To thoroughly clean the face you need something along with the water that will cut through the makeup and the oil but at the same time still be gentle and glide over the skin.

Find A Good Water-Soluble Cleanser

A good water-soluble cleanser is a terrific invention. It is a cross between a shampoo and a cold cream. What differentiates a good cleanser from a poor one is one that washes off the makeup without leaving the face dry (like soap) or greasy (like cold cream), contains no fragrance, coloring agents, abrasive particles and, most of all, is gentle to the skin. There are cleansers on the market that call themselves water soluble, but in actuality the instructions tell you to wipe the cleanser off with a wet wash cloth. Whether the cleanser is wiped off dry with a kleenex or wet with a wash cloth, that makes it anything but water soluble. Water-soluble cleansers replace the need for cold cream type products that need to be wiped off the skin. They also eliminate the need for soap, which can dry and irritate the skin.

Water-soluble cleansers are truly a pleasure. Imagine splashing your face with (tepid) water, then massaging a water-soluble cleanser evenly over your face, including the eyes, and then rinsing it off with more water. That even sounds refreshing. It is much more preferable than spreading greasy oily creams over the face and then wiping and rewiping them off with tissue or cloths. Doesn't that description feel messy and inconvenient?

SUMMARY: Water-soluble cleansers are a gentle, efficient way to remove makeup. Everything is done at the sink. Even a heavy-makeup wearer can take off all her makeup this way. I've been doing it for years. Using a water-soluble cleanser eliminates the need for a separate eye makeup remover, or boxes of kleenex to clean your face.

Okay, now comes the $64,000.00 question: How and where do you find a good water-soluble cleanser? It's an excellent question and I promise I will tell you, but please indulge me in an apology to those of you who bought the original version of this book. When I first wrote *Blue Eyeshadow Should Be Illegal*, I did not include the name of a water-soluble cleanser. I sincerely did not want to get into the product-recommending business. I felt that if my readers were informed of what to look for in a cleanser they would be able to find one. Sad to say, that was not anywhere near what happened.

After the first printing sold out, I received hundreds of letters asking me to name a specific cleanser. The letters repeatedly stated that there were no water-soluble cleansers available that met my requirements (no fragrance, no coloring agents, no oils, no strong shampooing agents like ammonia laurel sulphate) and the product needed to be gentle enough to use over the eyes without burning or irritating, and rinse off clean leaving the face feeling soft with no residue or dryness!

All those women who wrote me were right, finding a good water-soluble cleanser is a difficult task. I've only found one cleanser that meets all of those requirements and it is not a well-known product. In the second printing of the original book I finally gave in and added a paragraph that named a cleanser. In this updated version I am still recommending the same one; the cleanser is CETAPHIL LOTION from Owen Laboratories. Cetaphil has all the things I look for in a cleanser: It is fragrance free, has no coloring agents, it is relatively inexpensive, remarkably gentle and it removes all the makeup including eye makeup. You can find it in most drugstores across the country and around the world* in the pharmacy section. I'm sure there are other cleansers available that can do what Cetaphil Lotion does, so if you happen to know of

---

Internationally Cetaphil Lotion is always called Cetaphil; the only thing that will be different is the name of the company on the label. Overseas distribution is handled through a parent company of Owen Laboratories called Alcon.

one, please let me know and I'll be happy to share the information. For now, Cetaphil Lotion is the only cleanser I recommend.

Stress, Inflammation and Irritation

Perhaps by now you've noticed how emphatically I'm stressing the importance of being gentle and not irritating the skin. The crucial reason being gentle to the skin is so important is because of the skin's reaction to irritation of any kind. If I were to tell you that your skin reacts badly to stress, most likely you would agree with me, there would be little to argue about. Everyone knows stress can show up immediately on the surface of the face. Unfortunately the skin can react the exact same way to topical irritation as it does to internal stress. Skin can't tell the difference between stress and irritation, or pain and itching, it's all the same thing. It follows then that if stress is bad for the skin, so is irritation and the resulting inflammation. What physically happens when inflammation takes place as a result of irritation? The nerves react. That reaction triggers the part of the body the nerve ending is attached to. The nerves on the face are attached to the skin, hair follicles, oil glands, capillaries (blood flow to the skin's surface) and the underlying structure of the skin. If you activate the nerve endings by inflammation of any kind, the oil glands are going to produce oil, the skin can flake, and the blood circulation to the small capillaries near the surface of the skin will increase. This reaction can cause capillaries to break and become more noticeable. If there are surfaced capillaries already present on your face, irritation will make them redder. In short, irritation and cleaning the face do not go together. Irritate the skin and you end up with more trouble than you bargained for.

It logically follows that learning how to be gentle to your face is the most important part of skin care. There is no way you can even begin to hope for soft smooth skin when the face is being irritated every time you cleanse it. Irritation-free skin is the goal. From here on, I am going to help you eliminate those things that cosmetically beat up the face.

There are plenty of emotional and environmental stresses that bombard our skin all the time, some we can control, most we cannot: Crazy, intense work schedules, a frenzied home life, paying bills or your car breaking down are all potential problems for the skin. Extreme heat in summer (or in a sauna), extreme cold in winter and pollution during the entire year are worse. Wouldn't it be nice if we could control all these environmental irritants? I'm not suggesting that you can, but what I am suggesting is, if there are stresses you can control it makes sense to give it a shot. From my perspective, it is easier to eliminate the things we do in the name of skin care that irritate and inflame the skin than it is to control the environment or our emotional life. With that in mind, the following is a list of typical cosmetics and cosmetic ingredients to avoid. The skin can react stressfully to all of the following: astringents, toners, fresheners, hot water, cold water, wash cloths, scrub products, loofahs, buff puffs, most soaps, facial masks (particularly those that contain clay), saunas and any makeup items that contain alcohol, menthol, mint, eucalyptus, ammonia, phenol, and camphor.

SUMMARY: Think gentle! What makes this skin-care routine different from most others on the market is the theory that the skin doesn't have to hurt or tingle even a little to be clean. (If the skin tingles it is being irritated and inflamed, not cleaned.) The major rule for all skin types is, if it feels uncomfortable once, don't do it again. Pain and cleanliness have nothing to do with each other.

NOTE: It goes without saying, though I'll say it anyway, that my feelings about the ingredients I suggested you avoid are not widely shared by the cosmetic industry, dermatologists or pharmaceutical companies. They would argue that the concentrations of those chemicals are so low that the irritation is minimal. I would argue that what is minimal to them is not minimal for my face or yours.

They also would not agree with my sentiments about ingredients like camphor, menthol, mint and phenol. These chemicals are recommended because they are considered to be anti-itch ingredients. The theory works like this: Your skin itches. The nerve ending is begging you to itch. When you place these irritating ingredients over the itch the nerve hears the irritation message louder than it hears the itch message and interprets this as a reason to stop itching.

That reasoning is all fine and good if minor occasional itching is your problem. If it is not and those ingredients are used in facial skin-care products meant to be used every day, they will dry out the skin, create rashes and/or produce more oil. I am still convinced that those ingredients are a waste of your time and money.

No Bar Soap!

There are some problems with using soap no matter what type of skin you have. Actually I don't have to tell you that, because if you've used soap, and most of us have, then you already know it dries and irritates the skin.

Soap is primarily made of lard (tallow), lye or strong detergent cleansers. Simply put, lard can make you breakout and lye or detergents can be irritating, which may also cause you to breakout, flake or peel.

Lard is a fairly innocuous substance that doesn't pose as many problems for the skin as does lye, though there are those studies that show lard to be a troublesome ingredient. Tests have been done where a bunch of rabbits had their ears smeared with lard and after a period of time the little rabbits' ears started breaking out with blackheads and eczema. The lard in soap can potentially do the same thing on your skin. I know you think that when you wash soap off your face it is all being rinsed away, but that is not the case. Lard is not water soluble. The same soap (lard) film left behind on your tub or sink does not rinse off the face either. It is easily absorbed by your skin just like the ears of the rabbits. The lard being absorbed into the pore can clog it and cause your skin to breakout.

The other problem when using soap on your face occurs from the effect of lye or strong detergents. Lye, also called sodium hydroxide or potassium hydroxide, and detergent cleansing agents can burn the skin. What most of us believe is that the tight sensation we feel after washing with soap means our face is clean. You know the feeling I'm talking about, where if you open your mouth it pulls the skin around your eyes? If my skin feels squeaky clean the better off I am, right? Wrong! That feeling is irritated, dried-out skin, and nothing else.

The difficulty with asking someone to break a soap habit is that soap really does clean the skin thoroughly, too thoroughly! The positive of being over-clean doesn't outweigh the negative of irritated skin. After washing with soap, if you have dry skin you will have to run to your moisturizer or, if you have oily skin, the oil will resurface in about 90 seconds no matter how initially clean you feel. If you happen to have combination skin, you will reinforce that dual condition. Do yourself and your skin a favor and consider giving up soap for cleaning your face.

What about specialty soaps that come in clear bars, have non-soap-sounding names or contain creams and emollients that appear to have none of the properties of *regular* soap? Well all of that obviously depends on their individual ingredients. Some specialty soaps do not contain lard but do contain other forms of wax that keep the cleansing agent suspended in a solid form. Those waxes can absorb into the skin just like lard, and the cleansing agent in these soaps, even if it isn't lye, can still be drying and irritating. Creams in a soap might make the face feel somewhat less stiff after you rinse it off, but that won't prevent the irritation that the other ingredients may be creating.

Whether or not a bar soap is clear or has a non-soap-sounding name like glycerin or french milled, that does not tell you what it is made of. You can get that information only from the ingredient listing. If you feel some kind of bar soap is your only option then I would strongly suggest avoiding those that list tallow and/or sodium hydroxide in the ingredients.

SUMMARY: Use a water-soluble cleanser in conjunction with tepid water to remove your makeup or before you start your makeup. This is important to the skin not because it's natural or hypoallergenic or deep-cleanses, but because it's a gentle, thorough and inexpensive way to clean the face.

No More Astringents

A toner by any other name is still something you want to keep off your face. Whether it is called a freshener, astringent, clarifying lotion, witch hazel or sea breeze, and whether or not it has natural or *designed for sensitive skin* written all over it, these products irritate the skin, and do little else.

Let me set the record straight: **Astringents do not and won't ever close pores; they do not deep-clean pores, and they do NOT reduce oil.** Quite the contrary; because astringents severely irritate the nerve endings, they increase the oil production, which makes the pores larger to help accommodate the increased oil flow. A vicious cycle if you ask me. Astringents and toners worsen the very problem they were *designed* to handle.

The various types of toners available usually contain one or more of the following: alcohol, lemon juice, grapefruit juice, phenol, formaldehyde, menthol and mint, which will all burn the skin to one degree or another. Citrus in skin-care products like lemon and grapefruit extract is incredibly irritating to the skin due to its high acidic content.

In essence, stay away from all cosmetics that contain alcohol in any way, shape or form. There was some confusion in my first book about what form of alcohol you were supposed to avoid. Many cosmetics contain ingredients that sound like alcohol but they are not. For example, cetyl alcohol or alcohol esters are not the type of alcohol I'm warning you about. The ingredient label will list the alcohol you want to be on the look out for as "SD Alcohol", followed by a number. What's wrong with alcohol? Nothing if you're a surgical instrument. It is a great disinfectant for anything made of metal or plastic, but not for the skin. If you fell down and scraped your knee I'm sure you wouldn't grab your favorite astringent, much less the bottle of isopropyl alcohol in your medicine cabinet, to use on the wound. Besides, in order for an astringent (alcohol) to be an effective disinfectant, it needs to contain 60% to 70% pure alcohol. When you purchase an astringent you're getting mostly watered down alcohol in the 30% to 40% range with some other miscellaneous watery ingredients tossed in. At a 40% level you're not even getting an effective disinfectant, though you are getting an effective irritant. That tingly feeling is nothing more than irritation, and remember what happens to the skin with any kind of irritation.

Fresheners which claim to be gentle, or salespeople who tell you their toners don't contain that much alcohol, are misleading you. Diluted alcohol is still alcohol and even watered down, it is harmful to the skin. If the toner doesn't contain alcohol it will more than likely contain something equally as irritating, such as the ingredients I've mentioned earlier.

The only exception to this are the toners on the market that indeed DO NOT contain the harsh ingredients I've listed. They usually are a plain concoction of glycerin and water, accompanied by a fancy price, which won't irritate your skin, only your pocketbook. That doesn't mean it is *doing* anything positive for the face, but it definitely isn't hurting it either.

In all fairness though, toners and astringents can offer a way to remove the excess cleanser that doesn't all get wiped off or rinsed off. They can also help slough skin (remove extra skin cells that can block pores). While astringents can indeed serve that function, let me assure you that there are more gentle ways to deal with the problem of excess cleanser residue. Avoid buying cleansers that leave a film behind.

To Slough Or Not To Slough?

While you're tossing out your bottles of toners you might as well include your facial scrubs and abrasive sponges. These are the products that are advertised, along with those astringents, as being able to clean out pores. Cosmetic scrubs often contain tiny pieces of cement (silicon), fruit pits, seeds and other gritty abrasives or strong chemicals which are not going to clean out the inside of your pores. Remember, if you could get inside and clean pores out, as if you were a dentist drilling, you would be bleeding. The stimulation of the nerves which are attached to the oil glands simply produces more oil, thus refilling the pores. Now you have made the mythological deep-pore-cleansing situation worse. You're running your pores in circles.

These facial scrubs are also advertised as being able to slough-off skin. The major problem with products designed for this process is, who educated these peach pits to know the difference between a dead skin cell and a live skin cell? How can it tell when a skin cell is ready to come off or not ready to come off? The difficulty with these products is that you can easily end up scrubbing off more than is healthful for the skin. You can end up burning the face or ripping it to shreds, and then, by following up with your favorite astringent, burn it even more. The advertisements tell you this process makes your face feel clean and fresh. To them it may be fresh and tingly but to me, when I see red skin and feel tingly that's inflammation. If you want to feel tingly, fresh or look red and glowing, run up and down the stairs 10 times. I promise, you will not only look red, but you will have done something for your heart and lungs instead of just tearing up your skin!

Despite all those negatives about scrub products, they do not alter the fact that sloughing the skin DOES play a vital role in skin care. This sloughing action is a natural process the skin goes through; the cells from the lower layers travel to the surface layers where they die and are eventually shed. The cells that have made this trip are replaced by new cells that will, in time, have the same fate. In normal skin this process goes on incessantly and microscopically without your ever being aware that anything is happening. For other skin types it leaves havoc in its wake.

One of the reasons a pore gets clogged with oil is because skin cells that should be falling off the skin, instead fall into the pore and get stuck. The more skin cells that build up in the pore, the more they prevent the oil from flowing easily out of the pore. The skin which should be shedding itself on a regular daily basis is somehow held back. One of the things that is holding the cells back is the oil itself. Oil is a sticky substance that spreads over the skin, congregating mostly where the active oil glands are, in the center of the face. The oil works as an adhesive, keeping the shedding skin from going where it is supposed to go — off the face and onto the floor. The repetition of this occurring every day is when the problems show up. The skin cells build up, getting trapped by the oil in the pore, which causes the oil to back up and clog the pore.

Oily skin isn't the only skin type that may require help with shedding skin cells that stubbornly hang on longer than they need to. Dry skin can suffer from the same condition. The difference between the two is what causes the cells to back up and what those effects are on the face.

Dry skin has a problem with too much skin all wanting to be shed at the same time. One of the things that makes dry skin dry: Cells that are not ready to be shed lose their moisture before they're supposed to and, once the water is gone, these cells want to come off. Dried up cells want to be shed but if they're not near enough to the surface they can't do that. A dry skin backup occurs, and these waterless skin cells have trouble finding their way to the surface.

Most of the time, skin cells are very willing to give up their place in the cellular layers so they can be replaced by the cells that are plump with water. With dry skin, too many dried up cells are vying for the position of jumping ship and there are not enough water-filled ones to take their place. This crowd of cells each waiting their turn creates part of the backup. If you then put a moisturizer on top of those skin cells to reduce the dryness, the dried-up skin cells that want to be shed get additionally hindered under the oil/wax layer of the cream. To make matters worse, the more skin that is built up and unable to shed, the less able a moisturizer can function efficiently. The dried-up skin cells block the moisturizer from reaching the plump cells that are in danger of losing their water content. That's one complicated double-edged sword.

Cleansers that help slough the skin can prevent this back-up from taking place. The question isn't whether or not the skin needs help with this sloughing process, rather it is how much help does it need and how can you do it gently. I'll explain that more in the section that discusses how to use the baking soda.

Clearing The Oil Panic!

Oil is problematic. There is either too much or too little of the stuff and more often than not there is too much in some areas and not enough in others at the same time. Regardless of how much, too much is a problem in the pore. Oil paranoia is a media-induced fear that is hard to talk anyone out of. No one is ever going to feel comfortable while fighting the battle of breakouts. I'm not going to preach that you have to love your oily skin but neither am I going to encourage you to hate it. Somewhere there is a midground where you can learn to stop trying to rip it off the face and come to terms with a more gentle approach.

Oil on the face is needed to create a barrier between your

skin and the environment to prevent the air from absorbing the moisture from the surface of the skin. Those of us who have active oil glands never have to buy someone else's moisturizer; we were born with our own built in. Why some of us have more oil than others is another story that is lumped under the term genetics. You inherited that trait from your parents and the reason the oiliest areas on the face are the nose, chin, cheeks and the center of the forehead is because that is where we happen to have the most oil glands. There are fewer active oil glands as you get to the sides of the face. No wonder many of us tend to have a combination skin. It's the way the system works.

This is a good time to clarify what exactly all this *oil* is that causes so much grief on the skin. First of all the word *oil* is very misleading. From surface appearance we assume that the oil inside the pore is similar to the oil in mineral or olive oil bottles. That just isn't the case. The oil underneath our skin, in the pore itself, is hard. It is the same kind of waxy substance produced in our ears. This oil/wax, as it accumulates inside the pore, pushes its way to the surface liquefying at surface temperature. That explains the oil slick we sometimes experience on the surface of our skin.

The hard, whitish, wax-like substance secreted by our oil glands explains why excess oil production that gets backed up in the pore can stretch the pore and create solid bumps. The question is, how do you keep this oil flow from backing up?

The popular theory of *drying up* oil explains why there are so many alcohol-based products on the market for oily skin problems. The folly in this logic is that the alcohol makes the oil gland produce more oil and 90 seconds after ripping the oil off the skin, it resurfaces. You haven't changed anything.

One of the ways I recommend to reduce oil production is to calm down the nerve endings on the face. That means cleaning the face gently so you don't give the nerve endings anything to react to. (More specifics yet to come. Stay tuned.)

Twisted Logic

Before I delve further into the specifics of my skin-care routine, let's review what is happening when you follow the skin-care recommendations of many major cosmetic companies. Product specifics can vary from company to company but the basic routine goes something like this (you'll recognize it immediately):

First you wipe your makeup off with a cleanser that makes your face feel greasy. Following the cleanser, you're supposed to use an astringent to remove any remaining cleanser, which makes the face feel dry. Now the problem of dry skin is met by the moisturizer, which undoes the previous step. Finally, after you get your makeup on, you're told to powder the whole thing to undo the effect of the moisturizer and foundation. Now that you're not shining anymore (heaven forbid you should shine) you're sold iridescent eye shadows, iridescent blushes and shiny lip glosses so you can shine all over again. Get the picture? Buying products formulated to undo the previous step is a trap. This average routine, including cold creams, day creams, night creams, night cleansers, toners and/ or fresheners can cost anywhere from $45.00 to $150.00. And that total doesn't necessarily include scrubs, masks and other specialty items.

By comparison my alternatives and the products I recommend will cost you about $10.00. No matter how unconventional this might all sound to you, for $10.00 it's worth the chance that I just may know what I'm talking about.

After The Cleanser: Step Two

The last episode of this drama left you hanging perilously over the edge of your sink with the water-soluble cleanser rinsed off and your face dripping wet. Not a pretty site, but a perfect one to begin the next step with. This is the climactic revelation, where the heroine discovers what to do about all the sloughing information we dealt with a few paragraphs ago.

You will need to have a box of baking soda, Arm & Hammer or generic, opened and nearby, but not so near that the box can get wet and soggy. Pour some of the baking soda into the palm of your wet hand. Then, wherever you have blemishes, pimples or clogged pores, GENTLY massage a generous portion of baking soda over the blemished areas. If you tend to break out all over you can use the baking soda all over. If you have dry or sensitive skin, massage the baking soda briefly over the entire face avoiding those areas that are cracked, too tender or too dry and irritated to touch. Dry and sensitive skins must be cautious in how often and how gently they use the baking soda. The sides of the nose and the lip area can be particularly sensitive. All sensitive spots can and should be easily avoided. Listen closely to your skin and don't do what hurts. Once you've finished with the baking soda, thoroughly and generously rinse the face with water. Now you are ready to dry your face.

Baking soda, when wet, turns into a slightly abrasive paste that beautifully helps the skin remove those excess skin cells that sometimes need coaxing to do what they're supposed to do naturally. For skins that have problems with breaking out, baking soda, when massaged over a whitehead or blemish, will open up the lesion, which can aid healing. Sloughing also helps skins that breakout by further reducing the chances of the pore getting clogged with cells that have stubbornly refused to come off. Why *opening* up a blemish can help heal breakouts will be discussed further, in the section that deals with acne myths.

Those of you that are asking yourselves, "How can she say this about baking soda when she told me earlier to throw away all my abrasive cleansers? Baking soda, to say the least, is abrasive. She must have stock options with Arm & Hammer." I don't have stock options anywhere though I'm aware that it sounds like I'm asking you to add a different fuel to the fire, except I would never do that. This glaring contradiction has a logical explanation:

You're right, baking soda is indeed abrasive. Remember the discussion about sloughing skin? A certain amount of GEN-TLE sloughing action is good, if not essential, for most skin types. In fact, if oily skin that tends to breakout is going to find some relief from a cleansing routine, the baking soda is the foremost part of the routine. It is also essential for dry skin if the moisturizer is going to have an optimum effect. Also, if you take a closer look at some specific characteristics about baking soda, you'll discover it's by far more gentle than the scrubs you so diligently threw away after you read the last section.

Why is baking soda better than other scrubs? For three reasons. First, because it is a fine, even-grain substance and as a result is less likely to scratch the skin. Most scrubs contain uneven particles of ground-up earth, metal or seeds. This lack of uniform size makes the product more scratchy. Second, baking soda is an anti-inflammatory agent. One of the inherent properties of baking soda is that it reduces redness, irritation and itching. For example, when you get a bee sting you wouldn't put honey and almond pits on it, but you might use a poultice of baking soda to reduce the swelling. Last, because baking soda is NOT a grit suspended in a cream base, it contains no preservatives, coloring agents or waxes that can absorb in and clog the pore. For the money (89 cents for a medium-size box) you won't find a product on the market that works any more effectively. Always keep two things in mind when using the baking soda: **YOU CAN OVERDO THE BAKING SODA so DO NOT OVERSCRUB.** Judge how often you use the baking soda by listening to your skin. If your skin is dry and feeling very sensitive be ever so careful with your application and perhaps do this step only once or twice a week. Or you can mix some of the baking soda with your water-soluble cleanser and massage that mixture gently over the face. The cleanser will act as a buffer between your face and the more abrasive properties of the baking soda.

NOTE: Mixing the baking soda with a water-soluble cleanser should be done only with a cleanser that rinses off clean with no residue. If your cleanser is even slightly oily it will prevent all of the baking soda from being rinsed off, which can prove irritating to the skin.

ADDITIONAL NOTE: AS YOUR SKIN CHANGES, YOU CAN ADAPT YOUR CLEANSING ROUTINE TO ACCOMMODATE YOUR SKIN'S NEEDS.

After Step Two — Step Three

I know it's taken awhile to get through these steps, but at least by now you've dried your face gently with a towel and are ready for the non-aquatic part of the system. If you're still wondering what else you can do to help alleviate blemishes and blackheads you have come to the right step. What you will need for this part is a bottle of 3% hydrogen peroxide and cotton. With these two items in hand, soak the cotton ball in 3% hydrogen peroxide and then, wherever you have blemishes, apply it liberally to those areas. Be sure the cotton you're using is 100% cotton and not some synthetic facsimile.

You can buy 3% hydrogen peroxide almost everywhere: drugstores, grocery stores, convenience stores and pharmacies for about 69 cents a bottle. Although your initial reaction might be to think that 3% hydrogen peroxide sounds like it is too strong for the skin to handle, nothing could be further from the truth. Unlike your astringent, a 3% solution of hydrogen peroxide is an extremely efficient and gentle disinfectant. 3% peroxide can easily be used in place of any astringent, toner, freshener or like product and do far more for the skin without irritating it.

Hydrogen peroxide is an effective disinfectant at a 3% solution level — 3% peroxide to 97% water. Whereas alcohol, in order for it to be an effective disinfectant, needs to be at a 70% solution level. That makes alcohol useful only at a very toxic level. 3% peroxide isn't toxic at all. It is gentle enough to be recommended by dentists as a mouthwash to help prevent gum disease. You could never do that with an astringent.

3% peroxide does not burn or react on the skin unless the skin is abraded. Where the skin is opened the peroxide will fizz and turn white displaying it's disinfecting talents. Alcohol does just the opposite, it burns the skin upon contact no matter what is going on with it. 3% peroxide, with continual use, can change the color of blackheads by turning them back to white. (It does this by bleaching out the color of the melanin cells that have fallen into the pore, which turned the pore dark in the first place.) Alcohol just sits there on the surface of the skin and torments the nerve endings.

If you've been following all this up till now you may be wondering why there are astringents and toners in every skin-care line there is? I've wondered the same thing. Lord knows I've tried enough of them in the past, and one after the other all did the same thing — irritate my skin. My only excuse for this prior repeated abuse to my face is that those were the days when I thought irritation was making my skin better, even though it visibly looked worse. I kept hoping that would change and it did, but not because of astringents. My skin didn't have a chance back then.

Another question you may be asking is, "If the peroxide is so wonderful why don't the cosmetic companies use it in their products?" That's a very good question. The answer lies in the problem of product stability. Chemicals must remain stable and interact favorably with each other to make a cosmetic formula work. 3% hydrogen peroxide is a highly unstable ingredient. It can decompose upon contact with sunlight and air. That's why hydrogen peroxide comes packaged in those little brown bottles and should be purchased in small quantities, as it can break down very easily and become good old-fashioned water. On the other hand, alcohol, and any other cosmetic ingredient, is chosen for its ability to be mixed with practically anything and remain intact for long periods of time.

After painting such a rosy picture about 3% peroxide, as you well might have expected, there are two side effects you should know about before you start to use it: When using the 3% peroxide be careful with it around your hairline and eyebrows as it will turn the hair blonde if you repeatedly get it wet with the peroxide. Personally, I have adored the inexpensive highlighting along my hairline. My eyebrows used to be more of a nuisance. But I've learned to avoid those areas with the cotton and my hair is back to normal. For years I would tell people that I dye my hair and take care of my acne at the same time.

The second caution is that 3% hydrogen peroxide can be drying for those with ultra-sensitive skin and very dry skin. But the only reason those skin types should be using the 3% peroxide anyway is if they have a problem with blackheads or breakouts. If not, there is no reason to use the peroxide. If your skin is dry or very sensitive and has breakouts, use the 3% peroxide sparingly only over those problem areas. You can also dampen the cotton ball with a little water before soaking it with the 3% peroxide. The extra dilution should help cut almost any risk of irritation.

SUMMARY: 3% hydrogen peroxide is a good disinfectant for blemishes, changes the color of blackheads from black to white, causes minimal to no irritation on the skin, and it is even less expensive than the baking soda.

You Want Me To Use Milk of Magnesia Where?

For a while there you were almost convinced that I knew what I was talking about, until we got to this step, right? I understand, it sounds weird to me too and I've used it for years. But I promise, once I explain it to you it will make perfect sense. Well, maybe not perfect sense but it will become a more acceptable choice for treating oily skin and some types of acne.

For acne or oily skin I recommend you use milk of magnesia as a facial mask. (Aren't you glad I didn't mean for you to take it internally?) What could be in milk of magnesia that would make it suitable as a facial mask? All milk of magnesia is, is liquid magnesium. What is liquid magnesium? It's a simple combination of magnesium powder and water. When those two ingredients are mixed together they become magnesium hydroxide. Besides what it is traditionally used for, milk of magnesia has two other properties that make it useful for the skin: It absorbs oil and it is a very effective disinfectant. Exactly what you need when dealing with acne.

Here's how to use it: After cleansing with the water-soluble cleanser and the baking soda, or whether or not you use the baking soda, but before you use the 3% hydrogen peroxide, apply the milk of magnesia in a layer generously over the face. It can tend to be a little runny so be patient as you build up an opaque layer over the face. Leave this on till it dries, that should take no longer than 10 to 15 minutes, then rinse well. Milk of magnesia is difficult to rinse off so be sure to rinse thoroughly.

When I first started using my skin-care routine for oily skin and breakouts, because my condition was so severe, I used to use milk of magnesia under my foundation every day. I would use just a very thin layer placed over the skin. When it dried I would place my foundation over it. It did leave my face feeling *thick*, but that was the tradeoff for having my makeup last through most of the day without looking like an oil spill*. Once that super-oil phase of my life was over I stopped using the milk of magnesia every day and went to using it twice a week as a facial mask only. Nowadays I still use it, but only when my skin is acting up. How frequently you should use the milk of magnesia depends on how oily and/or

---

*If you are using a water-based foundation and you have very oily skin, you can try this for yourself to see if it works for you. It would work like some of the oil regulating lotions or creams that are on the market without any of the irritating ingredients. Do not wear the milk of magnesia under an oil-free foundation.

sensitive the skin is. The more oily your skin, the more often it can be used; the more sensitive your skin, the less frequently you should use the milk of magnesia, or you can leave it on for less time, say five minutes, before rinsing.

NOTE: Regardless of skin type never leave the milk of magnesia on overnight.

CAUTION: The 3% hydrogen peroxide and milk of magnesia are only to be used if you have a problem with blemishes and/or oily skin. If not, it is not necessary for you to include these items in your skin-care routine.

Everyday Normal Facial Masks

Those of you who won't be using the milk of magnesia may be wondering what type of facial mask is best suited for your skin. Most facial masks, whether commercially bought or handmade from food delicacies, are a waste of money and time. Next time you set out to buy a facial mask or concoct one yourself, consider the ingredients, and don't be fooled by promises that clay, french earth, vitamins, herbs, avocado or mayonnaise are going to do anything for you. Truthfully, I have no idea what positives can come from these masks. All these ingredients can do is sit on the face and waste your time, or worse, irritate your face.

Let me tell you for sure what I know masks can't do: **1.** You can't feed the face from the outside in (in other words you can't put liver on your face and have lunch). Nutrients can't be absorbed and used by the skin without being broken down by the digestive system. **2.** Plants or minerals left on the face can prove to be irritating to sensitive skins; this can hold true for the milk of magnesia. Be certain to rinse it off as soon as it dries or begins to feel even slightly uncomfortable. **3.** For the little bit of food or nature in a mask there are a lot of preservatives added to keep the product from molding and creating a new life form all its own.

There are exceptions to a mask's usefulness but that strictly depends on the ingredients. If you have dry skin and the mask you're considering contains oils, glycerin, petrolatum and other emollients and lubricants, I have to admit that it is indeed possible for facial masks to soften the skin, but not necessarily any better or differently than the moisturizer you use every day. There are no miracles and definitely no freedom from wrinkles, acne or dry skin from using them. These types of masks really provide no better results than what your daily skin-care routine should be doing for you every day.

Understanding Acne And Blackheads

If you're like me, you don't want to understand acne, you want to get rid of it. Why the face should have to erupt in such unsightly, swollen, red, white bumps or dozens of small black circular dots is beyond me. For most of us it is an embarrassment that all the makeup in the world can't keep a secret. The worst thing is that most breakouts don't occur on the sides of the face near the hairline — NOOOO! They occur in the center of the face right in the line of vision. Yes, this discussion doesn't thrill me, but it is nevertheless important if you are to understand how the 3% peroxide, baking soda, milk of magnesia and the theory of being gentle work together to be an effective line of attack against acne. The next few paragraphs describe how a pimple or/and a blackhead occurs. (You know, I hate the word "pimple".)

As was discussed in the section on sloughing the skin, one theory of why a blackhead occurs is that the oil (wax) in the oil gland (sebaceous gland/pore) backs up as a result of cellular debris that should slough off but instead sticks together and blocks the pore's entrance/exit. If this excess cellular material builds up it may stretch the surface of the pore, widening it, and filling it with more cellular debris. It was once thought that this accumulation in the pore turned black with exposure to air. Nowadays the theory leans toward the idea that some of the cells that have fallen into the pore contain melanin.

Melanin is the coloring agent of the skin that is naturally dark in color. Concentrated in a pore mixed with oil/wax, that color is exaggerated and appears black. Either way, like it or not, now you have a blackhead.

For a pimple to occur the same cellular debris would block the pore's entrance/exit and instead of enlarging the pore at the surface it would block the opening completely. The oil production would continue and further backup inside the pore at the base of the gland. This continuing oil production, which has no place to exit, can stretch the base of the oil gland under the skin. This swells the base of the pore beyond capacity, which can cause it to rupture. When this happens the oil/wax spreads over into the surrounding tissue and the skin becomes irritated. That creates further swelling and tenderness but not necessarily a complete pimple. Up until this point what you see on the surface of the skin is a red, tender bump that may or may not become a full-blown whitehead.

What is thought to create most whiteheads, separate from the redness and swelling, is the presence of a bacteria called propiobacterium in the same oil gland that ruptured open. The overproduced oil/wax that spilled into the tissue surrounding the pore is where this bacteria lives. When the wax invades the propiobacterium's territory the bacteria start gobbling up the wax. (Bacteria have to eat something!) This interaction between the wax and the bacteria produces an allergic reaction in the skin. This further inflames the skin. The inflammation attracts white blood cells to the area in a defensive maneuver, attacking the new irritation, and produces what we loathingly call a pimple. In other words, most pimples are really more of an overreaction by our skin's natural defense system to our own out-of-control oil production. The reason baking soda is effective in fighting acne is because it helps with the skin's sloughing process, which reduces the chances of the dead skin cells sticking together, remaining on the surface of the face and blocking the pore's entrance/exit. 3% hydrogen peroxide works because it can kill the bacteria culprits which are making matters worse when the oil gland ruptures. The 3% peroxide does this without further damaging the skin or exciting more oil production. The milk of magnesia absorbs the excess oil that is in the pore, retarding potential backups.

This basic rationale for dealing with acne is not new. Many skin-care routines and products on the market are based on this theory. The difference is that many over-the-counter remedies for acne, even though they may contain ingredients that kill bacteria to some degree, and perhaps degrease the surface of the skin, they also irritate the skin at the same time, which causes the problem to recycle itself. At the least my routine can do the same thing without any of the irritating side effects. Acne is already red and irritated; it would be nice for a change to do something for the skin that doesn't make it more red and irritated.

NOTE: Please be aware that nothing gets rid of blackheads and acne 100%. Nothing except reducing or stopping oil production, which is possible with the prescription oral drug called Accutane. This form of medical treatment for acne will be discussed at length later in this chapter.

By the way, an occasional pimple now and then does not make a case of acne. I can't tell you how many women I've talked to with one pimple on their chin who inform me they have an appointment with their dermatologist that week. That's truly overreacting. What happens to skin sometimes, regardless of age, race, sex, diet, or religious preference, is that it breaks out and there isn't much a doctor, a cosmetic company, or the routine I've explained here can do to change that. Hopefully what steps 1 through 4 offer is a course of action you can take when you do break out that helps retard the process.

Acne Myth 1

"Mostly teenagers get acne." I used to think that as well until I turned 30 and it was still there. After the age of 30 I became resigned to the idea that my tendency to breakout wasn't ever

going to go away. I was going to grow old, wrinkle, and under my wrinkles there would be pimples. Oh well, that's life.

Women and men at any age can get acne. It tends to be a problem equally distributed between both sexes during adolescence, with teenage boys having the slight edge. As we get older the likelihood of men being plagued with post-puberty acne is less than it is for women. That's probably because of the volatility of female hormones, but there is little medical understanding of why hormones play a role in acne — what is known is that they do. If they had asked me, I could have told them that too. Like clockwork, since I've been 11, one week before I get my period the revenge of the pimples strike vengeance on my face anywhere they want to.

Acne Myth 2

"Don't squeeze that." This is not a fun topic, but someone's got to handle it. Whether or not you use all of the skin-care suggestions I recommend for acne, or you use the products available at the drugstore or the department store, once you get a pimple, if you don't remove what's inside, it will take twice as long to heal no matter what else you do. The reason the skin is swollen, red and painful is because of what is inside the pore. Depending on the severity of the lesion, when you remove the oil/wax and white blood cells that have formed the pimple, the swelling will go away almost immediately. The more severe the blemish the more difficult it will be to remove. Whoever told you that squeezing blemishes would automatically cause scarring, or would damage the skin or brain in some way, was wrong. What is true, though, is that the way you go about squeezing a blemish can cause damage. The method you use to squeeze the blemish is where the trouble can lurk.

I'm not the first person who has suggested that you have to open a lesion and remove what is inside to get rid of it, but I might be one of the first to describe exactly how you should go about it. For those of you who aren't interested in a graphic description of how to do this I would skip to the next section. For those of you who are interested, the blow-by-blow is what follows: 1. Squeeze blemishes only after washing the face and preferably after massaging with baking soda and using the 3% hydrogen peroxide. The baking soda will help remove any skin that might be an extra hindrance covering the pore's opening. 2. Be sure the face is completely dry. 3. You can use your fingers covered with kleenex or not, whichever is easiest for you is fine. 4. Be sure that your fingers are placed evenly on either side of the lesion around the borders of the reddest area. 5. Begin squeezing with even pressure ever so gently in a downward direction and then slowly move in toward the center of the lesion with a final gentle push up. The operative words here are gentle and even pressure. 6. If the blemish does not give easily, stop squeezing and try again. You may want to try placing your fingers at a different angle around the blemish before you try squeezing again. **NEVER TRY SQUEEZING MORE THAN TWO OR THREE TIMES.** Over-squeezing damages the surrounding skin and that is what can create ugly scabs and scars. 7. **NEVER** try to pick or scratch the blemish open. This will also cause scabs and scarring, and healing will take even longer than if you had left it alone.

   REMEMBER: Leaving the pimple alone is best if, after a gentle massage with baking soda, gentle squeezing won't remove anything. NEVER OVER-SQUEEZE. If the built-up oil/wax and fluid inside the blemish can be easily removed, it is a great way to help promote healing. If it can't be easily removed, and you continue to squeeze anyway, it is a great way to have scabs, scars and a general mess where you used to have only a blemish.

Doctoring The Skin

After a brief but honest roundtable discussion with a group of business people I respect a great deal, who just happen to work predominantly with dermatologists, I realized how I was going to rewrite this chapter. The first thing I knew I would have to do is admit that the way I handled this section on dermatologists in the original version of *Blue Eyeshadow* was a little, well, how should I say it — hysterical — and, well, possibly unprofessional too.

Back in 1984, when I wrote the opening paragraph for this chapter, I stated honestly that the subject of dermatologists was a loaded issue for me. I had strong feelings about how skin doctors dealt with and treated their patients who had acne or eczema. I based that on my numerous experiences as a patient of a dozen or so different dermatologists and the information I collected from 10 years of working with women on their skin-care and makeup needs. That was valid information but only a part of the whole story. The other part of the story that I did not adequately research were the patients who were satisfied with their dermatologist's care. I was probably so biased at the time that I just assumed there weren't any. This version of *Blue Eyeshadow* will present both sides.

The fact that this is a loaded subject for me hasn't changed. What has changed is my attitude and perspective. It is true that I still have issues with many aspects of dermatology, and I have concerns about the way some dermatologists treat their patients. What my boardroom friends pointed out to me is that those issues are really no different than any other complaints you've read from other consumer writers about the medical field in general. And those complaints are always escalated when doctors are dealing in an arena, like skin, where so little is known about the cause of the problems that the doctors are asked to treat. The patient and the dermatologist are both likely to be frustrated when that kind of dilemma is present. I should know, I was one of those frustrated people and I met more than a few frustrated doctors.

Growing Up With Acne

Growing up with bad skin wasn't easy. Before I went to bed at night the one thing I remember always praying for was to have good skin. There were times my skin was worse than others but it was always on the edge of disaster. My humiliation knew no bounds. Big ones right in the center of my forehead or on the tip of my nose giving way to a collection of medium- to small-sized ones driving me nuts on my cheek or chin. My memory seems to have registered that I was the only one I knew with acne. I know that can't be true but the feeling is one of distinct isolation. And it was lonely. Who cared that my acne, as far as I was concerned, was a terminal disease. From the age of 11, along with the advent of puberty, my hormones and whatever other factors were in play ruled my self-confidence.

For years my parents shlepped me from one dermatologist to the next. At the age of 18, when I had moved away from home and was out on my own, I started taking myself. By the age of 24 I had seen at least 18 different dermatologists who had prescribed varying remedies that, from my way of looking at things, didn't work and cost me more than I could afford. In those days it was $25.00 a visit, about the same for the medication and they always wanted me to come back every two weeks.

Each visit to a new dermatologist's office resembled the last. The doctor would look at my hands (I also had severe eczema on my hands) and my face and then write a prescription. Once in a while they would stick dry ice on over a blemish or two and *then* write a prescription. The prescriptions involved one or all of the following: I was to wash with whatever soap I wanted, though Zest or the like was preferable. The next step was to use Cleocin Lotion — an alcohol-based solution of the antibiotic clindamycin, as the disinfectant and then Retin-A (bet that one rings a bell) as a topical irritant that would help keep the pores from getting plugged. Often this skin-care program would include my regularly taking oral antibiotics*

---

* *Oral antibiotics for many women can cause vaginitis, which sends them directly to their gynecologist for yeast infection medication.*

and the regular use of a scrub product like the buff puff. The doctor would then tell me to come back in two weeks, where the scene seemed to repeat itself. The entire interaction never took longer than five to seven minutes, if that. This would continue for a few more visits, until I gave up and decided to brave it on my own till the next friend recommended a new dermatologist that they heard was supposed to be good. With a medical history like that, is it any surprise I have strong emotional viewpoints concerning dermatologists when it comes to acne?

Somehow back then I thought that acne was my fault. My face just wasn't clean enough. That if I washed it one more time, or a little harder, it would make a difference and my face would clear up. When I would use an astringent or the Cleocin Lotion, the Retin-A and the buff puff, I thought the more it burned the more it must be working. The burning was a sign to me that it must be killing whatever it was that was making me breakout. If someone had only told me that acne and blackheads had nothing to do with being dirty, and clearing it up had nothing in the world to do with pain, I would have been grateful. Well, at least now I know different and so do you. Those days are over. Onward to the new irritation-free days.

After The Days Of Accutane

I should make it clear that almost all of my experiences with dermatologists were before the days of *Accutane* and before the days when they had developed less irritating combinations of Retin-A. It was also before the days when many doctors had already stopped prescribing antibiotics as the primary treatment for acne. And thank goodness, to a certain extent, things have greatly changed. Not that all dermatologists are going to handle you with kid gloves, but equipped with the right information and questions, you may improve your chances of getting what you need.

Accutane is an oral drug that can perform miracles for many people with severe acne. It is a derivative of Vitamin A that is taken by mouth in pill form. If you have severe chronic acne please discuss its use with your physician. Accutane is extremely risky and is used only for chronic severe acne; it is not recommended for everyday acute acne. (Not that acne is ever *cute*.) Acute acne differs from chronic acne in the intensity, size and frequency of how you breakout. Acute acne may cause minor scarring whereas chronic acne refers to large break-outs that can permanently distort the shape and appearance of the skin.

Be sure to completely go over Accutane's side effects with your physician, step by step. You need to know what you can do for any of the complications that can occur before you make a decision to use it. Accutane can cause brittle bones, back-aches, liver and kidney problems, very dry skin, blood cell problems, and it can also cause miscarriages and fetus deform-ities. This is a very serious drug that needs to be dealt with in a well-informed, cautious manner.

WARNING: ACCUTANE HAS A VERY IMPORTANT WARNING! IT CAN CAUSE SERIOUS PROBLEMS FOR PREGNANT WOMEN. MISCARRIAGES AND SEVERE BIRTH DEFECTS HAVE BEEN ASSOCIATED WITH TAK-ING ACCUTANE. IF YOU ARE PREGNANT OR ARE CON-SIDERING HAVING A BABY YOU SHOULD NOT BE TAK-ING ACCUTANE. Accutane carries a strong warning label carrying this information. Unfortunately, many women and doctors have ignored this warning. Or, if this warning wasn't taken lightly by the prescribing doctor, there were additional risks involved because Accutane is frequently prescribed to young people who are not always careful or aware of the responsibilities of birth control. The other problem is that many women have started taking the drug who did not realize at the time that they were pregnant. If you are sincerely interested in trying Accutane to help eliminate the disfiguring effects of chronic acne, then it is essential you either consider using some type of birth control or abstain from sexual relations altogether until the Accutane therapy is complete.

It would be a good idea for you to know how long you will need to be on Accutane, and how much the entire therapy costs. Accutane therapy can be very expensive. You will also need to make repeat visits to the doctor to check on your progress, monitor your blood count and keep track of what is happening to you physically. Accutane is not something you would ever want to take without ongoing supervision from your dermatologist. You may want to find out ahead of time if your medical insurance covers Accutane therapy. For those of you who can use it, it can indeed *cure* cases of acne that, prior to the days of Accutane, used to leave many with no hope of having anything other than disfigured, scarred facial skin.

Retin-A For Acne

Retin-A as a topical cream/gel for acne has been around for a long time. It can be a viable option for many women with acute (there's that word again) acne. When I first tried Retin-A years ago I personally found it too irritating to use and I have received dozens of letters from other women who have also tried Retin-A for acne and found it too irritating. I am presently giving it another try in conjunction with my skin-care routine and the information I've gathered about the different types of prescriptions that are available. This time around though, I'm not necessarily using Retin-A for my acne as much as for the benefits the skin can derive from its anti-sun damage and anti-cell-aging properties. I have chronicled what that day-to-day process of applications has been like in Chapter 5.

To say the least, Retin-A can definitely cause dermatitis along with mild to severe skin irritation for most people. The severity of that irritation can be exacerbated by what else you use on the skin to clean it. Extreme sensitivity can be caused by using the Retin-A in combination with other skin-care items, prescribed or over-the-counter, such as: astringents, wash cloths, scrubs, oil control lotions, alcohol-based products and soaps. Some of these items may have even been recommended by your doctor. The lack of concern or interest for treating the skin gently, while still treating acne at the same time, is sometimes less obvious than it should be. The effect of this insensitivity is that the skin can become red, dry, cracked and still remain oily and blemished. Not a pleasant alternative, especially when some of the irritation can be avoided.

Another reason why our experiences with Retin-A may have been uncomfortable is because of the strength of the prescription that was doled out. Retin-A comes in different potencies. They are as follows: Retin-A Liquid 0.05%, Retin-A Gel 0.01%, Retin-A Gel 0.025%, Retin-A Cream 0.01%, Retin-A Cream 0.05%. The gel and liquid forms of Retin-A are both alcohol based. The cream form is mostly a combination of waxes that suspend the Retin-A in a more lubricating, nonirritating formula. As you can probably guess by now, I would never encourage anyone to use the alcohol based forms of Retin-A. Whatever irritation you are likely to experience from the Retin-A itself will be increased by the irritating effects of the alcohol in the gel and liquid bases.

Doctors may automatically prescribe the strongest percentage gel or liquid form of the Retin-A for their patients who have oily skin. Not all doctors are savvy to the different percentage strengths of Retin-A that are available on the market or the differences in their base ingredients. Those physicians who are aware of these differences often disagree with my concern about alcohol on the skin. They may feel that alcohol increases absorption into the skin. My feeling is that alcohol evaporates too quickly to make that a truly viable reason to use an ingredient that can cause such adverse reactions on the skin. It wouldn't hurt for you to encourage your doctor to write a prescription for the lowest strength cream base of Retin-A.

You may be surprised how open he/she may be to your suggestion. If your skin reacts favorably you can always move to the stronger percentages next time you need a refill.

Another way to deal with the irritating side effects of the Retin-A is to reduce how frequently you apply it until you build up your tolerance. To achieve the maximum benefit, it is best to use the Retin-A twice a day if you can tolerate it. If your skin proves too sensitive for that, another alternative you can try is to use the Retin-A once a day or every other night. If these precautions don't work you can mix half the amount of cream you use each night with an equal amount of the Cetaphil Lotion. This will dilute the compound and make it easier to use on the face. In the long run though, studies do seem to indicate that with time the skin can build up a tolerance to the effects of the Retin-A. What initially proved terribly irritating when you first began treatment, can eventually stop all together.

To combat the irritation as it shows up, instead of reducing the frequency of application, ask your doctor to write a prescription for a cortisone cream that can be used on the face and eyes. The cortisone can be used in spot areas and can quickly and effectively stop the irritation in its tracks. After a while, as your skin adapts to the Retin-A, you will probably be able to stop using the cortisone cream altogether and use the Retin-A twice a day with no problems at all.

Of course, you can always stack the cards more in your favor by using the safety net of applying Retin-A in association with a gentle skin-care routine, which can greatly minimize its irritating side effects. A good way to prepare the skin before you begin using the Retin-A is to stop using all abrasives on the face (including the baking soda) two weeks prior to usage and be sure that you are only using the Cetaphil Lotion as your cleanser. This way the skin will have a less likely chance of having any topical abrasion that may compound the irritating effects of the Retin-A. If you continue to breakout, even while using the Retin-A, massage only the blemish with the baking soda. Be careful not to massage the baking soda all over as frequently as you did before.

Cleocin Lotion

The topical antibiotic Cleocin Lotion is a very popular prescription that dermatologists use hand-in-hand with Retin-A. The Cleocin Lotion is a mixture of the antibiotic clindamycin dissolved in alcohol which is then used as an astringent. Technically the Cleocin Lotion works along the same theoretical line as the 3% hydrogen peroxide or the 5% or 10% benzyl peroxide. All three get into the pore (sebaceous gland) and work to kill the bacteria that is hanging-out in there which could be creating your blemishes. Supposedly the Cleocin Lotion, because it contains a strong antibiotic and is suspended in alcohol, is considered to do a more thorough job than the 3% peroxide or the 5% and 10% benzyl peroxides.

As you already know I would never agree to the rationale about using alcohol as the base, but for the sake of argument let's say the Cleocin Lotion does penetrate better than the peroxides and kills bacteria more thoroughly; the question then becomes how much penetration do you really need when the problem is so near the surface? Why use that strong of an antibiotic on the skin when the 3% peroxide may work just as well and for less money? After all, once a bacteria is dead it isn't necessary to kill it again. In short, I'm just not convinced the Cleocin solution works any better than the 3% hydrogen peroxide. But again, for the sake of argument, let's say the Cleocin Lotion does work better and you can afford to use it along with the subsequent repeat office visits, the other problem with Cleocin Lotion as I mentioned above is the alcohol solution the antibiotic is suspended in. As a result, for the sake of getting an effective disinfectant you get an incredibly strong, and I mean strong, irritant. Whatever the benefit of the increased effectiveness of the antibiotic, you once again worsen the situation by leaving the skin inflamed, oilier and dried out.

There is an exception to the complaints I have about the Cleocin Lotion which would nicely negate everything I just said. Sad to say this alternative is not widely used. The exception is that the Cleocin Lotion can be made primarily with the Cetaphil Lotion I talked about earlier in this chapter. What the dermatologist does is write a special prescription that instructs the pharmacist to dissolve the clindamycin tablets in a minimal amount of alcohol and then mix that solution with the Cetaphil. The lotion is mostly the very gentle nonirritating Cetaphil and the antibiotic itself with little to no residual alcohol.

Unfortunately, there are those dermatologists who are not sympathetic to the discomfort or problems that are caused by alcohol or other irritants on the skin. They have no problem recommending that their patients who have problems with blemishes use soap, buff puffs, Cleocin Lotion and strong solutions of Retin-A all at the same time. But now that you know more clearly what your options are you can find the gentle choices on your own or you can encourage your doctor to treat your skin more gently from the start.

What To Ask Your Doctor

If you find that the skin-care routine I'm suggesting for acne doesn't work for you or you just want to give your dermatologist a chance in conjunction with the ideas you've read so far, keep the gentle things we've been discussing clearly in your mind. This way you will have a basis on which to evaluate your skin-care options with the doctor. I'm including a list of questions and ideas that can help when you go in for your appointment and the doctor recommends some of the things we've been talking about:

1. Find out how long your appointment will last. The longer the better. If at the time of the appointment you have

serious questions about the prescriptions you've been given talk to the doctor or nurse. The nurse not only has good information, she oftentimes is more sympathetic and patient.

2. Ask the doctor what you're supposed to do when irritation occurs. Hopefully the suggestion will be to either cut back the frequency of use or you can be given a weaker strength prescription which can replace the original.

3. Ask if it's possible for you to bypass a return office visit if you're not experiencing any difficulties. Hopefully the doctor will let you check-in by phone to say that you're doing okay and then give you a refill if needed at that time.

4. Be sure to get a thorough explanation of how the prescriptions you will be using can affect your skin in the sun. Read the instructions back to the doctor so that you are sure you understand everything.

5. Take notes while you are with the doctor and bring your questions with you. You don't want to leave the appointment feeling like you wished you had asked a dozen things you forgot while you were there.

SUMMARY: Whether it is decided that you go on Accutane therapy or topical Retin-A and Cleocin Lotion it would be wise to use the Cetaphil Lotion as your water-soluble cleanser when you wash your face. The major drawback to both these skin-care prescriptions is that they can render the skin exceedingly dry and irritated. Cetaphil will clean the skin and not dry it out any further. You will find that most soaps on the market will leave your face painfully dry. The same is doubly true if you are using any products that contain alcohol. The combination of these prescriptions with soap (even so-called nonirritating soaps), scrubs and alcohol-based cosmetics can kill your face. I would encourage you to avoid anything on the face that can cause unnecessary irritation, such as: astringents, all bar soaps, wash cloths, kleenex, scrub products (at least not all over the face), facial masks, hot water, and any products that are designed to *dry up acne*.

A Just-In-Case Checklist

This is a practical checklist to make sure you've double-checked all the possible things that may be aggravating your acne besides your skin-care routine. Although most acne is not solely caused by allergies to food or cosmetics it can be made worse by both. (If I just look at a moisturizer, any moisturizer, I breakout immediately.) To help avoid or at least somewhat curb these factors that could be compounding the problem be aware that any of the following can be trouble for those of you who have severe to mild forms of acne:

1. Allergies to milk fat or dairy products in general. Although, generally speaking, diet DOES NOT affect acne, there are a few foods that have been known to cause skin reactions. Chocolate, however, is not one of them, unless of course it is milk chocolate and you have a problem with milk.

2. Allergies to shellfish or any other suspect foods or food groups. If you are curious to see if a particular food group is the culprit, simply stop eating all forms of whatever it is you want to check out for two to three months and see what happens. If you stop for shorter periods of time and your skin clears up, that may be coincidence rather than fact. Your skin needs time to see what happens to it over the long haul.

3. Problems with fluoride in toothpastes, especially if you're just breaking out around your mouth and chin. If you suspect this is true for you, check with your dentist and try brushing with baking soda and 3% hydrogen peroxide instead of toothpaste for a while and see what happens. The American Dental Association recommends the combination of baking soda and 3% hydrogen peroxide as a way to fight bacteria build-up in the mouth.

4. Irritation from your partner's beard, particularly if you're just breaking out around the chin and mouth. This is definitely a problem for women with sensitive skin.

5. Not getting all your makeup off at night. If you have a problem with breaking out and you sleep in your makeup, I assure you, you will have a problem with increased breakouts in the morning.

6. Certain cosmetics, like foundations, moisturizers or cream blushes. Especially if the lesions are occurring only where you place those items.*

Test your sensitivity to any of these potential allergens by eliminating them one at a time and watching the results for a few months. It may make a marked difference in the appearance of your skin.

---

*You may have read that certain cosmetic ingredients are known to cause acne. These studies, which have been widely reported on in the past, have a credibility problem. The studies isolated the suspect ingredient and tested it on rabbit ears in its pure form. That's all fine and good except that in most cosmetics you rarely find these ingredients in their pure form or in any significant amount at all. That still doesn't mean your foundation or blush might not be a problem for you, but it may or may not be because of the ingredients you've read about. In fact you are more likely to have allergic reactions to the perfume or fragrance in your cosmetic than you are to almost any of the other ingredients. When in doubt stop using the cosmetic in question for a period of time and see what happens.

Chapter Five

The World After Retin-A

I Told You So

It isn't considered polite to say I told you so, but I've never been known for my gentility, so forgive my brashness as I calmly exclaim, I told you so! For years I've been talking around the country insisting at the top of my lungs that there aren't any wrinkle-free scientists up in the Swiss Alps inventing miracle potions for grown-up skin that can keep it from growing up — and that is STILL the case, there aren't. What has changed is that now there is Retin-A, which, according to scientifically published research as documented in the *Journal of the American Medical Association*, can visibly alter and reduce the effects of SUN-INDUCED DAMAGE and WRINKLING. But that doesn't make Retin-A some cosmetic prodigy or secret; just the opposite is true. Retin-A doesn't come in the form of a cosmetic, it is not a miracle, secret ingredient that you can't comprehend, and it doesn't cost anywhere near what you thought a cream like this was supposed to cost. What is true is that it does need to be prescribed by a doctor, you do need to be careful how you use it, there are some negative side effects and it has limitations that are logical and understandable. Isn't that a refreshing, honest difference from a product that really can potentially change some of the wrinkled appearance of the face?

Science, in its infinite capacity to expand and produce miracles, has, for the first time in the history of cosmetics and pharmaceuticals, finally created a topical cream that seems to eliminate, change, alter and in general get rid of the wrinkling caused by the sun. In short, all the gimmicky slogans plastered on cosmetic wrinkle creams can probably be slapped on this stuff and it would be closer to the truth than ever before. How times have changed. After years of putting up with hormone creams, the natural and vitamin craze, the 1980s' absurdity with collagen creams and whatever other fad ingredients with technical-sounding names came along, finally there is a light at the end of the tunnel.

The technical name of this serious drug is retinoic acid or topical tretinoin. Last year this product would not have received any recognition or reaction from anyone. The only people who knew about this stuff were dermatologists and their patients who had acne. For almost 20 years dermatologists have been using it as a prescription for acne. Even these doctors had no idea what Retin-A could do for *photoaged* skin, they only knew how it could help their patients with acne. If you read the section on Doctoring Your Skin, you already know my feelings about Retin-A for acne; it can be incredibly irritating and cause dry, flaky, red skin. Those warnings can be even greater when using Retin-A on mature skin. But if you can handle it, you have absolutely nothing to lose and everything to gain. Besides, if you have problems with breaking out, your skin may clear up at the same time you work on eliminating wrinkles.

What I have done so far is very quickly paint a broad, overly simplistic picture of this new phenomenon. As you may well expect by now, I would never leave you that poorly informed. Before I carry on anymore about Retin-A as a potential, honest-to-goodness anti-wrinkle cream I would like to discuss what is true about dry skin so that you can stop wasting your money on the absurd cosmetic wrinkle creams that are out there doing little more than decorating cosmetic counters all over the world. It is important for you to understand why wrinkling and dry skin are not related, and therefore why all the other so-called wrinkle creams on the market could not in a million years do what they said they could do.

To organize this complicated conglomeration of ideas and issues I think it best to follow this order: **1.** Look at the dynamics that separate dry skin from wrinkling and explain what can truly be done for dry skin. **2.** Examine the differences between the wrinkles that occur due to photoaging and the wrinkles that occur due to genetic inherited aging. **3.** Describe the particulars about what is available or desirable in a moisturizer. **4.** And last but not least, what do you do now that Retin-A is available?

Face Up To The Truth

Moisturizing the skin is one of the most emotion-packed, sensitive issues I can think of in skin care. The emotions get involved because our egos get hooked into wanting the impossible. Wrinkling is a hard-core visual sign of our own mortality, which is not the most wonderful thing I can think of. It is more wonderful to think of preventing that. It is understandable why we steadfastly want to believe that if we use a moisturizer we can prevent or at least slow down the inevitable process of wrinkling. I would like to believe that too but it's not the truth.

Even if the subject of wrinkles wasn't so emotionally sensitive, the issue impacts almost everybody regardless of race, religion, sex or ethnic background. That's because at some point most everybody is going to wrinkle to one degree or another, which is radically different from most other skin conditions. Wrinkles will never just get up and go away by themselves. If you grow up and use your face or walk outside, you are going to get wrinkles and even Retin-A can't change all of that.

Another reason moisturizers are such a loaded subject is because of the misinformation that accompanies this well-advertised group of products. The cosmetic industry *wants* you to believe that their moisturizers can change or prevent wrinkling by reducing dry skin. Or in reverse, they want you to be very concerned about preventing dry skin and, by association, if you stop dry skin your wrinkles will be stopped, reversed or slowed at the same time. If you accept their premise you will need to use their creams and potions from the moment you become an adult, till forever. This long-established myth overrides all other information. There probably aren't many women out there who have any idea of what they're buying when it comes to a moisturizer, other than the fallacious notion that it will impede or negatively affect the wrinkling process. Even those of us who understand the truth of what moisturizers can really do, oftentimes continue to buy wrinkle creams anyway. There must be something deep inside of us that refuses to realistically deal with the truth:

THERE ARE NO **COSMETIC** CREAMS OR LOTIONS YOU CAN PURCHASE THAT WILL CHANGE, ALTER, AFFECT, PREVENT OR DECREASE THE WRINKLING PROCESS OF AGING ONE IOTA.

QUALIFYING STATEMENT: The only cosmetic cream that can affect wrinkling is one that contains a **SUNSCREEN** and in that case it is a preventive treatment that protects the face from the sun and nothing more. If you are using Retin-A that will change some types of wrinkling, but you will not find Retin-A in a cosmetic. **YOU CANNOT FIND RETIN-A IN ANYTHING BUT A PRESCRIPTION FILLED BY YOUR PHARMACIST.** Many cosmetic companies will tell you that their product contains vitamin A or a derivative of vitamin A which they will insist works just like the retinoic acid (a vitamin A derivative) that you find in Retin-A. That simply is not true. The vitamin A used in cosmetics is radically different from the vitamin A acid found in Retin-A.

In all due respect to my readers, there is a totally reasonable reason why you believe the unbelievable, and that is primarily because of brainwashing. The cosmetic industry has spent a lot of money convincing you that dry skin and wrinkling are associated. It is that basic, otherwise harmless and erroneous supposition that has created all this insanity. If that line of reasoning, that dry skin and wrinkles are related, were true then it would indeed make sense to buy a moisturizer and expect it to take care of wrinkles. And yet nothing could be further from the truth: Dry skin and wrinkling have nothing to do with each other. Let me say that again:

DRY SKIN AND WRINKLING HAVE NOTHING, I REPEAT, NOTHING, TO DO WITH EACH OTHER!

I know that's hard to believe. After all, if what you've been reading are fashion magazines, which all advertise to death the myth about wrinkle creams, or you've collected trad- itional or natural beauty books, which often concur with the former, why should you believe me? They've been telling you for decades the opposite of what I'm trying to tell you. Besides, from a logical point of view, on the surface and strictly by association, what they've been telling you makes sense; both dryness and wrinkles appear on the surface of the skin and both can get worse as you grow up. BUT, the similarities and associations start and stop there. These are the facts:

DRY SKIN IS CAUSED BY THE INABILITY OF THE SURFACE LAYERS OF SKIN TO RETAIN WATER AND THAT DEHY- DRATION DOES NOT AFFECT OR IMPACT HOW A WRINKLE IS MADE.

WRINKLING IS SOLELY THE RESULT OF CHANGES OC- CURRING IN THE UNDERLYING LAYERS OF SKIN AND THE STRUCTURE OF THE SKIN CELL CAUSED BY SUN DAMAGE, FACIAL EXPRESSIONS, GENETIC PREDISPOSI- TION AND GROWING UP, WHICH HAS NOTHING TO DO WITH DRY SKIN OR THE AMOUNT OF WATER, OIL, OR MOISTURIZER PRESENT ON THE SURFACE.

POINT IN FACT: If the opposite were true, if dry skin and wrinkling were associated, then 10-year-old kids with dry skin would wrinkle, and they don't — they wait till they grow up just like we do. Also, if dry skin and wrinkles were con- nected then women with oily skin would never wrinkle, and, as I can personally and professionally attest to, we do.

Dry Skin vs. Wrinkles — Separating The Evidence From The Process

For the purpose of review and comparison, the dynamics of dry skin go something like this: A skin cell, during its life span, for some unknown reason, travels from the lower layers of the skin to the surface layers where it is eventually shed and replaced by the cells in line behind it making the same trip. During this migration, the cell, hopefully, retains its moisture content to the last moment until it reaches the surface of the skin and jumps off. When dry skin conditions are present, what changes is that the cells waiting in line to be shed, lose their moisture content way before they reach the surface. When this happens the cells all want to come off at the same time and they can't. They can only come off when it's their turn, not at the moment when they lose their moisture content.

Why some skin cells retain their moisture and others lose moisture (i.e., dry skin patches or dry areas) and why some people have dry skin, and others do not is not fully understood. It is theorized that something may be genetically wrong with the cell wall, which protects the moisture content inside the cell. Another theory is that there may be a genetic tendency for the oil glands to not produce enough oil or any oil at all to protect the cells from the dehydrating effect of the environment. To make matters worse, both of these factors, defective cell walls and nonproductive oil glands, may be present at the same time. It is also a mystery why dry skin gets worse as we get older. It seems that the same inherent problems that seem to occur in dry skin show up as we age even if those problems weren't present before. What they know for sure is that moisturizers temporarily prevent dry skin from happening — why dry skin happens at all remains a genetic puzzle.

Wrinkling is another story altogether. Wrinkles involve a few different processes that may or may not be happening at the same time. One of the primary causes of wrinkling is the deterioration of the support layers of the skin.

The support layers of skin are called by those recognizable cosmetic buzz words, collagen and elastin. Well, at least they were important buzz words in the early part of the '80s, but just like every other cosmetic fad ingredient their claims and promises never panned out. Collagen keeps the skin taut and elastin allows the skin to spring back to its original shape. The deterioration of the collagen and elastin does not take place as a result of moisture loss because these cells do not go through the process of migrating to the surface of the skin and shedding. Rather the breakdown of these cells occurs because of sun exposure, genetics, gravity and facial expressions. Dry skin is loss of cellular moisture, wrinkling is the deterioration of collagen and elastin for reasons other than dehydration.

Genetic Aging vs. Photoaging

One of the facts of life seems to be that we are genetically preprogrammed for most of our youthful support systems to break down as we get older. Much like the dry skin that shows up later in life, some wrinkling also comes from an inherited preprogrammed breakdown. With genetically caused wrinkling what happens is that at some point the collagen and elastin gets tired of doing its job and relinquishes its responsibility of holding things up, therefore, things like laugh lines, furrowed brows, jowls, sagging necks (have I depressed you yet?), pouchy undereyes and hanging eyelids, flabby underarms, etc., etc., all happen to one degree or another as we age.

Genetic preprogramming is not the only cause for the collagen and elastin breaking down and creating wrinkles. The other biggy is the sun, what nowadays is referred to as photoaging. The radiation from the sun really does a number on the face. Radiation in accumulating amounts destroys the collagen in the supportive layers of skin making it thinner and weak. On the surface of the face just the opposite happens, sun radiation causes this area to become thicker creating furrowed ridges that overlap and look heavy. Over time, with consistent exposure to the sun, enough thinning of the lower layers of skin and enough thickening of the surface layers will have taken place that eventually all the leathery signs of sun-damaged skin will become evident.

Photoaging differs in appearance from genetically pre-determined wrinkling in form, texture and placement. Sun damaged skin is not necessarily the sagging skin around the jowls or laugh lines. Photoaged skin is most apparent on the cheeks in an accordion-like pattern that is thick, heavy and sallow in color. In actuality sun-damaged skin can occur wher-ever the skin has been exposed on a daily or regular basis to the sun. Sunbathers are not the only ones subject to the effects of the sun, though they are more likely to show damage faster and more severely. The damaging effects of the sun can happen just from the rays we get from walking outside, to driving in the car and everything in between. To poignantly point out this difference between the two please take the following inti-mate test:

THE BACKSIDE TEST OF RECOGNIZING THE DIFFERENCES BETWEEN PHOTOAGING VERSUS GENETICALLY PREDETERMINED AGING

This test is best taken by women over the age of 50. If you're not that age yet, next time you're at your local health club, you can give this test anonymously to any woman who you know or think is that age or older. Simply adapt the rules as you go.

Here's what to do: Next time you find yourself completely naked and in proximity of a full-length mirror stand in front of it, and take a good look at yourself. Next, examine the skin's appearance on your face, hands and neck. Then, examine the skin on your buttocks and entire backside. Now compare the differences between those areas. From this point on you want to try and be as totally objective as possible putting all personal feelings on the back burner. The test is most revealing when you take note of exactly the way the skin looks in terms of tone, color, elasticity and texture.

NOTE: If weight is not a problem for you and your backside is slightly rippled with cellulite, just ignore that. But if you are 30 pounds overweight or more you are not a good candidate for this test. Fat cells have a tendency to plump the skin and give it a fuller look than someone who is normal weight. In that case use someone else's body to take this test.

What you should notice is that the skin on the buttocks is fairly even in color with minimal to no signs of sallowing, ashenness or any other appreciable color changes. You should also notice that the skin here has lost some amount of its firmness. There might be stretch marks present or the skin may appear to be hanging. This would be particularly noticeable nearer the thigh area.

The face will be more sallow (Caucasian and Asian skin) or ashen (black skin) in color. Even if there are surfaced capillaries present the skin will still lack an overall pink or golden glow. This glow would radiate evenly from the skin itself instead of from irritation or the irregular blood flow from the surfaced capillaries. Laugh lines around the mouth and sagging lined skin on the lid and undereye may also be present. There will also be crows' feet around the eyes and some accordion like lines in the area between the cheek and the jaw. These accordion-like lines may be somewhat leathery in appearance. After taking note of all this you will have noticed by now that there are none of the leathery, accordion or crows' feet type of lines present on your backside as there are on the face.

The major differences between the skin on the face that gets the most sun and the skin on your backside that gets the least, would be this recognizable difference in color and the accordion-lined wrinkling that shows up around the lower cheek area and the eyes. Obviously the face will show genetic patterns of aging, facial expression aging and photoaging. It is what the backside doesn't have, namely this accordion wrinkling, that the face does have that typifies sun-damaged wrinkling.

Now that you understand the difference between photo-aging and genetically inherited aging you can put your clothes back on and finish this chapter. How Retin-A fits into the scheme of things will soon become clear. There are a few more topics that need to be understood before I get to the specifics about Retin-A.

Miscellaneous Wrinkling

By the way, there are two other miscellaneous causes of wrinkling you should know about, one is caused from repeatedly pulling at the skin, and the other is from everyday facial expressions. Unfortunately only one of these can be avoided or altered to prevent the side effects from an otherwise harmless activity.

Repeated manual stretching of the skin or the pull on the skin that is present all around us from gravity can cause the skin to sag by putting too much tension on the elastin support fibers. Much like a rubberband the skin can only take so much before it can't take any more and gives way. This effect is most evident in women who wear heavy earrings. With time the constant pull will cause the ear lobes to sag. The same is true if you constantly pull at the skin by repeatedly wiping off makeup with kleenex or a wash cloth. The pull on the skin from this type of cleansing routine is one way to help stretch out the elastin fibers and cause them to sag. That is why I recommend water-soluble cleansers so you never again have to wipe off your makeup. Stop pulling at the skin and you avoid one way the skin can age. As you already know intuitively you can't do anything about the effects of gravity itself on the skin; standing on your head will only cause the skin to stretch in the other direction.

The other type of wrinkling is caused from facial expressions. That doesn't mean you should stop using your face, quite the contrary, the more expressive the face, the more attractive you will be perceived. But there are unnecessary facial expressions that can be avoided which definitely increase lines on the face: Pursing the lips while smoking can cause fine lines around the mouth. Frowning or furrowing the brow will crease the forehead. Squinting will create lines in between the eyes. And facial exercises will compound the whole situation and make it worse. The skin that is supposedly exercised during facial aerobics is the same that is used when you use your face anyway. If you move the skin more you risk stretching the skin more and creating more lines. Believe me there aren't any bulging cheek or jaw muscles that will change facial lines.

One More Time: The SUN WARNING

A few additional words on the sun and your skin. Even though it's boring and you've heard it a thousand times before one more time won't kill you. Sunshine directly on bare flesh ages the skin, dries the surface layer, makes the skin look leathery, breaks down the supportive skin fibers and is generally worse for human skin than almost any other element in our environment (with the exception of gravity and Chicago in the winter, which we can do nothing about). Here's the scary part: 500,000 people every year will develop skin cancer and that number is growing. The statistics suggest that one out of every seven Americans will eventually be affected by skin cancer. According to the Skin Cancer Foundation, between 90% and 95% of all skin cancers can be traced directly to sun exposure. In spite of how awful that sounds, most skin cancers are completely curable and preventable. But that takes awareness and information.

Suntanning ads would have you think otherwise, but then they're trying to sell tanning oils, aren't they? A very practical, although obnoxiously dull idea, is to avoid exposing your skin, especially your face, to direct sunlight. If you simply cannot avoid being in sunlight, and who can or wants to do that anyway, use a good sunscreen that contains PABA or some other sunscreen ingredient (there are plenty on the market) and continue reapplying every few hours. This need to reapply is very important, **SUNSCREENS DO NOT LAST ALL DAY, THEIR EFFECT WEARS OFF WITHIN A FEW HOURS** depending on the Sun Protecting Factor number (SPF) of the product you're using. Also be sure to reapply your sunscreen immediately after swimming or exercising. There are waterproof sunscreens that do not wash off immediately when you get wet, and seeing as how you can burn right through the water while swimming that's great, but they still need to be reapplied.

SUGGESTION: If outdoor sports and athletics are the way you spend time, including running and cold weather sports, be sure to carry a tube of chapstick or clear lipstick that contains a strong sunscreen. This is a convenient easy way to glide protection over the face any time you need it. Plus, the consistency and ingredients in the chapstick and lipstick are great at protecting the face from the wind as well as the sun.

The all-important SPF number is something most of us understand and use correctly when we go to purchase a sunscreen. It is the number on sunscreen products that indicates how much sunblock you're getting. For example, if you use a sunscreen with an SPF of 8, it would take 8 times longer for you to develop a burn in the sun than it would normally if you did not use a sunscreen at all. What a sunscreen does is let you stay longer in the sun without being adversely affected by the sun's rays. The higher the SPF number the more potent the protection. To reinforce the significance that is associated with using this rating system the following are some specifics you should memorize and remember always:

1. Use a sunscreen liberally. When it comes to sunscreens a lot is better than a little.

2. If you plan on wearing a hat or spending your time in the shade and you think that will protect you from the sun, think again. Things like sand, snow, water and even concrete can reflect the sun's rays from the ground directly onto your face.

3. Clouds and haze pose harmful problems for the skin. They filter out all the sun's rays except the ultra-violet burning ones.

4. Do not forget the ears, lips, underarms, tops of your feet and balding scalps which are also subject to sun exposure. These areas can be prime targets for the sun and are often passed over as we diligently apply sunscreen to other areas of the body.

5. Sunscreens do not alter past sun damage and sun damage starts from the first time you walk outside. From very young everyone should wear a sunscreen. Infants, children and teenagers can solve future problems from happening by starting now.

6. Wear a sunscreen every day on those parts of your body that get exposed to the sun, particularly the face. Makeup, unless it contains a sunscreen, will not protect your face from the sun.

7. Certain medications including birth control pills, tranquilizers, antibiotics, Retin-A, etc., are possibly phototoxic, which means they are dangerous to use in conjunction with prolonged sun exposure. Check with your physician before using these prescriptions and sunbathing.

8. Skin cancer in the beginning stages may show up as a slight skin discoloration or an irregularly shaped or discolored mole. If you notice anything that you suspect may be a problem ask your doctor. It may save your face!

9. The warmer the climate the greater your chances of skin cancer.

I Almost Forgot — This Is Step Five

I hope those of you with dry skin weren't feeling left out. In spite of the fact that I left moisturizing the skin to last, most everything that has been explained so far applies to your skin as well. Even though dry skin may be your primary concern, at one time or another you will also be likely to have trouble with breaking out, irritation and all the other side effects of cleaning the face, using makeup and having skin in general that affect everyone else too.

The basics of the water-soluble cleanser and the baking soda as I described before, are both very important for alleviating dry skin. The water-soluble cleanser is essential because it cleans the face gently without drying it out. The baking soda is just as important because it helps the skin cells slough off which also helps the moisturizer penetrate better to reach the skin cells that have not as yet lost their water content. Even the 3% hydrogen peroxide can be used as needed when blemishes choose to show up. The milk of magnesia probably will never be necessary for you unless you happen to be one of the few women who breakout and have a very oily skin and dry surface skin at the same time. Although, almost without exception, that type of combination skin is often caused by the way the skin is cleansed rather than by an inherent problem with the skin itself.

By now you have a pretty good idea of how to wash the face and what things you need to avoid like the plague if smoother skin is to be a plausible reality. But for now, what you really want me to settle for you is, after your face is clean what do you use next? Given the myriad of moisturizers inundating stores that sell cosmetics, what do you use for dry skin and how do they work?

After this lengthy prologue the answer may be more simple than you want to hear, but here it is anyway: If you don't have dry skin you DO NOT, I repeat, you **DO NOT** need a moisturizer. If your skin is dry you DO need a moisturizer. All any moisturizer can do for you, to one extent or another, is retain moisture in the skin and protect the skin from the environment. No more and no less.

Honest, if your oil glands are doing their job you don't need a moisturizer. If your oil glands can't keep up with your dry skin then you need a moisturizer. But there is nothing life-threatening about a woman over the age of 25 not using a moisturizer. Your skin will not wrinkle any faster as a result of this oversight on your part. Your skin will actually fare better if you don't load it up with unnecessary creams and lotions. Too much oil, whether it is yours or someone else's, can make you break out and prevent skin from sloughing.

That's the full extent of it. There aren't secret laboratories somewhere in the Swiss Alps or in France, with wrinkle-free scientists who have packaged the fountain of youth for only $400.00 a pound which figures out to $25.00 an ounce. The more expensive the product does not mean there is any more hope inside the cream waiting to live up to its claims. Nowadays we read in earnest the articles about live cell injections* or placenta extracts swimming around in creams with miraculous rejuvenating properties. We confuse the legitimate medical research that is presently being studied that involves aborted fetal tissue for treatment on certain diseases with the promises of what a cosmetic says it can do when the ingredient listing suggests it contains something similar. The cosmetic product

---

*Speaking of live cell therapy, I was on a talk show once with a gentleman who seemed to be the guru of live cell therapy. His evidence and support material was almost satirical. It was hard to believe that he actually took himself seriously. He spouted fancy technical-sounding words wrapped in a European, scientific-looking medical complex with absolutely no shred of credibility or legitimate research anywhere to be found that substantiated his claims. All the statistics he quoted were from movie stars who had discovered his clinic and loved the results. Well, that's scientific proof isn't it? If George Hamilton loves it, it must be good, right? All any of that proves is that Mr. Hamilton can waste his money along with anyone else if they so choose.

does not and legally cannot contain anything of the kind. Even if a cosmetic could include cells or placenta extracts by the time the product was cooked, packaged and shipped the cells would be completely ineffective. Medicine is medicine and cosmetics are cosmetics and never the twain shall meet.

What's In That Stuff?

Back to moisturizers: Regardless of price or brand name, moisturizers can benefit the skin by counteracting the effects of evaporation and helping to keep water inside the skin cell. It does this by supplying the skin with oils and waxes. The oils and waxes smooth over the top of the skin preventing the air from drinking up the water within the cell. The oil in the moisturizer technically is replacing the oil your oil glands may not be supplying for you. When you buy a moisturizer you are purchasing some type of oil other than your own, to replace what your skin doesn't have.

The statement that moisturizers put water back into the skin is not accurate if at all true. The water in a moisturizer is primarily used to mix with ingredients called emulsifiers to create a creamy smooth appearance. By the time the water touches the skin it is quickly evaporated and gone, way before it ever has a chance to absorb into the skin. Given the price of water and its function of making a moisturizer pleasing to use, it is not surprising to find water the number one ingredient on the label.

On the other hand, the statement that the oil in a moisturizer substitutes for someone's inactive oil glands to help keep the water in the cell from evaporating is a completely accurate description of what moisturizers do. Oil is the other primary ingredient in moisturizers. Regardless of how expensive the cream is or what the claim written all over the label says the first ingredients will always be water, oil or/and wax. Not very fancy, but true nevertheless.

Now here's a good question: If most moisturizing creams are oil and water, and they are, why don't they look like oil and water? Answer: It is the wax-like thickeners and emulsifiers that are added to the mixture which turn the water and oil into the traditional creamy form you're used to buying. The exclusive formulas you're rubbing into your face are mostly comprised of water, oil, wax, some preservatives, coloring, fragrance, and for the sake of marketing, the latest miracle ingredient like placenta, collagen, elastin or vitamin A. There are also the all-important ingredients that help the cream spread nicely over the skin and keep the cream from changing shape in varying temperatures. The three major ingredients, water, oil and wax, are the crux of a moisturizer and you need to know more about them in order to understand what you're buying.

Water, Oil And Wax —
The Real Secret Ingredients

What are the secrets of these not-so-secret ingredients? Let's start with the universal basic — water. Whether the water in a moisturizer is purified, extracted from some plant, such as aloe, distilled or ionized it is still just water. Whatever benefit was supposed to be derived from the specialty of the water would be lost after the product was cooked, perfumed and preserved. Even if the properties of the *special* water remained intact after the product was finally put together, the skin doesn't need special water and for the most part the skin cell isn't capable of absorbing it anyway. The purpose of water in a moisturizer is to give the product its texture. Even if the water in the moisturizer could absorb into the skin, fancy water wouldn't stay in the cell any better than plain old everyday water. The skin cell doesn't care what kind of water it is.

The oil component in your moisturizer is a little more complicated than the water component. Basically whether it is olive, shark (squalene), peanut, sesame, coconut, almond, cod liver, Vitamin E, lanolin or mineral oil, it is still just oil. The difference between oils exists between the vegetable or animal oils, and the synthetic oils better known as mineral oil or petrolatum.

Mineral oil is an excellent moisturizing ingredient. It's possible that you've heard different, but I can't tell you why mineral oil has gotten such a bad rap. Whatever negatives are thought to be connected with it don't change the fact that mineral oil serves a major function in moisturizers by keeping the environment off the face. Mineral oil is made of a very large molecular structure. The size of the molecule prevents the mineral oil from being absorbed into the skin. Because it can't be absorbed it stays on the surface of the skin and prevents the surface cells from loosing their moisture content. Vegetable oils have a smaller molecular structure which is more compatible with the skin. The smaller molecular size of the vegetable oils make them more easily absorbed into the skin. Once the vegetable oils have been absorbed, they can protect the skin cells that haven't made it to the surface yet from losing their moisture content too. The problem with vegetable oils is that they tend to go rancid in cosmetic creams. There is no reliable way to prevent that from happening, so the cosmetics that contain vegetable oils always have to contain fragrance to cover up the rancid smell. Even though mineral oil does not have the rancidity problem that vegetable oil does, mineral oil by itself is not as desirable as when it is accompanied by a vegetable oil.

This problem of needing an oil, like vegetable oil, which absorbs nicely into the skin yet tends to go rancid is easily corrected by using animal oils, or vitamin E oil (tocepherol), in place of the vegetable oils. The most widely used animal oil is lanolin, which nicely absorbs into the skin and has no problem with rancidity. Lanolin and vitamin E oil (which is an oil and NOT a nutrient on the surface of the skin) works as a wonderful compatible counterpart to the mineral oil. As you begin to become more aware of ingredient listings, you will indeed start noticing that almost all moisturizers contain mineral oil and lanolin as their major components because of the very reason I just discussed. Vitamin E is somewhat less popular, but it is not any more or less desirable than the lanolin, so you needn't worry about vitamin E's lack of availability in moisturizers.

The wax group of ingredients come in a multitude of forms that can be either synthetic, such as by-products from the manufacturing of alcohol or petroleum, or there are natural waxes such as beeswax and tallow. Yet regardless of its form, wax is wax. Well, that last statement is not one hundred percent true. There are huge differences between different types and grades of waxes. Waxes do a lot more than just thicken a product. Technically, they also help keep it stable and give the cream some of its texture and form. Different blends of waxes do not resemble each other. That is why even though the cosmetic ingredients in moisturizers tend to be more or less the same they do not always look or feel the same. Formulas do differ but the formulation does not add any extra hidden benefits. The feel of a moisturizer is a personal choice. What feels comfortable and soothing for your skin is what is best for you.

Collagen — Yesterday's News

This is another brief *I told you so*. Collagen as a cosmetic ingredient placed in moisturizers works the same as lanolin and mineral oil do in a product. It keeps moisture in the skin, but no better and no worse than mineral oil or lanolin. Collagen is not a miracle. It is just another way to keep moisture in the skin. Do not spend extra money on a product just because it contains collagen, it is a blatant waste of money if you do. Collagen injections are something completely different from the collagen inside of cosmetic moisturizers. For the particulars on collagen injections refer to the section *To Lift Or Not To Lift*.

SUMMARY: When buying a moisturizer check to be sure that the product you are considering contains mineral oil, and lanolin, vegetable oil or vitamin E. You also want to avoid fragrance, coloring agents and long ingredient lists. Here are some inexpensive moisturizers that meet my requirements and are readily available in most drugstores:

Neutroderm — for slightly dry skin and those of you who are allergic to lanolin; this product is lanolin free.

Lubriderm — for almost everybody who has skin that tends to be a little to somewhat dry.

Eucerin Lotion — for very dry skin.

Apply the moisturizer over a clean face that is slightly damp. Do not rub the moisturizer into the face, that stretches and irritates the skin. Smooth your moisturizer evenly over the face and allow it to absorb into the skin.

NOTE: You do not need to use bottled or canned European water on your face. These pricey atomizers offer nothing special that cannot be simulated by wetting the fingers with tap water and transferring that to the face. Making this simple step more complicated and costly is one more way the cosmetic industry lies in wait with gimmicks that are designed to appeal to your esthetics and not the benefit of your skin.

Reading Between The Lines

None of what I am about to tell you is going to sound surprising so forgive me while I beat a dead horse to death: The cosmetic industry takes full advantage of our fear of aging. Their ads imply that their products can do the impossible, which they can't.

When you buy a moisturizer ignore all the advertising rhetoric. Pick up the package and read only the ingredient label and nothing else. If you do not find at least two or more oils in the first several ingredients, of which one should be mineral oil and the other lanolin or vegetable oil, you'll end up buying a lot of water and wax, and you need the oils and water, not the wax. Actually, wax is an important ingredient, but it is not essential for the skin, it is essential for the product.

Specialty moisturizers are an amazing marketing creation. Eye creams, throat creams, night creams and wrinkle creams never contain anything really unique and different that can do anything above and beyond what your daily moisturizer can do. When you finally analyze the truth behind the rhetoric, it is still just a moisturizer that does what every other moisturizer does, which is keep water in the skin.

If there is something different about specialty creams it may be that they contain an extra oil or a blend of waxes that gives the product a more creamy texture. For the most part, in terms of wrinkles, any cosmetic cream besides your daily moisturizer or sunscreen is totally unnecessary. If you have exceedingly dry skin and you need more protection at night, using almost any form of pure oil can replace a specialty cream. Economically and reasonably speaking you can skip the extra waxes in the fancy creams and just use the oil. In other words simply use your daytime moisturizer at night and place a pure oil over the drier areas wherever they show up.

NOTE: If you have a problem with eczema-like patches of dry skin or irritation on your face that persists regardless of how much moisturizer you use, especially if you've been using the water-soluble cleanser and not overscrubbing with the baking soda as well, you can purchase one of the over-the-counter cortisone creams. Place the cortisone cream on after you use your moisturizer and use it only on the irritated areas. If this doesn't help you may want to consult a dermatologist who could prescribe a more potent cortisone cream for those problem areas.

REMINDER: Being born female and being over the age of 21 does not automatically mean you need a moisturizer.

You do need a moisturizer for dry skin but don't buy someone else's oil when your skin produces enough of its own. Oily skin doesn't need a moisturizer at all as it has its own built in. No one needs more than one reliable moisturizer regardless of the time of day or night she chooses to wear it.

SUMMARY: No matter how much you moisturize your skin, you have little or no control over the inevitable wrinkle. The inevitable is determined by your parents, your suntanning habits, the effects of gravity on your skin and whether or not you repeatedly pull at the face. What you are capable of doing for the skin is reducing superficial dryness and reducing photo-aging with the use of a sunscreen and Retin-A. If the skin is dry, a moisturizer simply makes the surface of the skin look smoother and softer temporarily until more is needed.

MY MOST SINCERE RECOMMENDATION: Take all the money you'd ever spend on cosmetic wrinkle creams and put it in the bank. Then by the time you're in the market for tucks, lifts or injections the money will be there with interest.

To Lift Or Not To Lift

The entire subject of medical/cosmetic surgeries and procedures poses more questions than just the ones that meet the eye, and it is perhaps those questions that have nothing to do with what we see that are the more difficult ones to answer. The typical questions cover what types of procedures are available and what are the results, both negative and positive, that can be expected from these medical anti-aging solutions. Perhaps the first question we should be concerned about has nothing to do with technicalities: Why do we want to do all this restructuring to ourselves? Why can't we just be all right the way we are? It's a provocative notion to examine why so many of us want to cut, inject, or rub away those things that are neither dangerous nor lethal to our health.

It could be explained simply by repeating the standard one-liner of, "If people want to look better and younger, and modern medicine can provide that vehicle, why not?" Asking why not begs the question. That answer is not only simplistic, it avoids looking at the personal aspect of what these surgeries/ procedures can mean for the individual. If we stop and look inside, turning to a more intimate introspection, that answer would run the entire spectrum of emotions for each of us who has ever wondered what our face would be like minus a sag or a line here and there.

I'm assuredly not the most qualified professional to discuss the philosophical, sociological and, ultimately, psychological issues that are involved in this subject. However I understand that sociologically we live a lot longer than we did a mere 75 years ago, which means we have a lot more aging to put up with than ever before. Philosophically I earnestly believe and know that we are fine the way we are but we also live in a society that puts a great emphasis on personal appearance. There have been enough studies conducted which clearly demonstrate that the better you look, the longer you live, the more successful you can be, and the greater the chances are that you will receive preferential treatment wherever you go. And finally, I'm all too aware of the emotional impact caused by living in a world that is preoccupied with the surface, while deemphasizing who we are inside as human beings. How all of that affects us is vastly complicated. Somehow it seems easier to ignore that, schedule an appointment and take your chances.

Those issues are indeed the more meaningful ones that surround medical alternatives to aging. In spite of this long discussion I have no answers or suggestions that can point the way through the personal and social decision process of choosing whether or not any medical/cosmetic procedures are indeed for you. Use these thoughts for consideration and reflection as a beginning step to assist you in making a decision.

In the long run I'm really neither pro nor con cosmetic procedures that alter the effects of aging. I am wholeheartedly impressed with the skill of a surgeon or doctor who can create the appearance a woman may have always hoped for. Yet, I am also equally concerned that a woman may believe these procedures will imbue her with some type of happiness or gift of instant self-esteem. The gift from things like collagen injections or face lifts is nothing more or less than physically what they can change on the surface of the skin. The energy for enjoying life cannot be stitched into a face, nor can the perplexities of day-to-day stress be smoothed away by filling in wrinkles. As cliche as this may sound it bears repeating, especially for those of you who are on the threshold of considering a medical/cosmetic procedure or two: Joy and happiness are not purchasable commodities. The passion of living a wonderful existence comes from within and only you can make that a reality — you and your zest for finding and giving beauty to the world around you.

Filling In The Lines

After telling you that moisturizers, facials and facial exercises do nothing to change how the skin wrinkles, having pulled the *wrinkle-free* cosmetic rug out from under you, let me make my way back into your good graces by mentioning a few things that can change the appearance of those wrinkles created by genetic inheritance, facial expressions, gravity and the sun.

The medical/cosmetic options that are available to anyone who wants to, and can afford to permanently or semi-permanently, depending on the procedure, change her appearance are mind boggling. What is even more overwhelming is how simple to miraculous the alternatives that exist can be. Whether it be a simple desire to straighten a nose or plump up a sagging laugh line, to a major reconstructive effort such as resetting an accident victim's cranial structure back to normal, the world of cosmetic medicine is doing things you might not have given a passing thought to just a few years ago.

Nose jobs, chin implants, cheek implants, eye tucks, orthodontics, jaw restructuring, collagen injections, and face lifts are some of the more common cosmetic/medical procedures you've probably read or heard about. As you already may know each one of those options by themselves can produce incredible results. When you consider the endless possible combinations, in the hands of the right team of experts, almost any look, within reasonable limits, could be attempted and perhaps realized.

Before I start sounding too much like an ad for cosmetic surgery let me quickly put the above elaboration into perspective. I am not encouraging anyone to run out and get their teeth wired or their cheeks lifted. What I'm doing is sharing my astonishment at what is happening out there in the cosmetic/medical arena. I did not intend for this book to be a reference guide for those of you who need consumer-oriented information about cosmetic surgeries. What I did research were the more everyday cosmetic procedures that are done in a few minutes in your dermatologist's or plastic surgeon's office for a relatively small expense and potentially little risk. Those procedures were collagen injections and Retin-A. For more definitive information about the other options a plastic surgeon or orthodontist might offer, please look at the auxiliary book list.

Collagen Injections

A wrinkle or scar occurs because the collagen, the support tissue of the skin, breaks down. Collagen injections, not collagen creams, temporarily build up the skin's depleted collagen supply by reintroducing pure collagen back into the skin. When the collagen is injected into your skin it is readily accepted by your system and actually takes on the characteristics of the surrounding tissue. Injectable collagen actually becomes a functioning part of your skin and can possibly stimulate the production of new collagen.

Collagen injections can diminish laugh lines, frown lines, acne scars and lines around the mouth. Collagen injections do not necessarily replace the need for cosmetic surgery. For example, injections cannot be used on sagging jowls or drooping eyelids. They are also never used for the treatment of the lines under the eyes, "ice-pick" type acne scars or scars with sharply defined edges. But for the lines and scars it can be used on, the results will blow you out of the water. As for what age group can consider collagen injections: If you have a wrinkle or a scar that is suitable for injections how old you are makes no difference. The entire procedure for collagen injections takes place in your doctor's office (dermatologist or plastic surgeon) with relatively little discomfort and in a remarkably short period of time, then presto, for a period of time, anywhere from six months to three years, depending on your skin and the type of collagen that is used, no more wrinkles until the next injection. The need for repeated injections is due to the nature of the injected collagen. The injected collagen behaves so much like your own collagen it is eventually depleted and needs to be rebuilt up to maintain the desired effect.

Retin-A: What Do You Do Now?

You could start by impulsively jumping on the bandwagon and making an appointment with your dermatologist or physician to request a prescription for Retin-A, say a two or three months' supply, which you could then quickly fill at your local pharmacy. Once you got the tube paid for you could then run home and start smearing the stuff all over your face and wait impatiently to see the sun's fury erased forever from your skin. Then, in about a week or two you would most likely be witness to the most inflamed, red, and dried out skin you may ever experience in your whole life.

On the other hand, you could start by taking time to gather the necessary information you will need to make an informed decision about whether or not this treatment is something you want to be involved in. Once that was done you could then make a rational decision to give Retin-A a try, which would also allow you time to carefully prepare your face for the treatments and plan what action you will take if irritation does occur. That would be my preference and hopefully yours.

Although I understand the urgency of wanting to get some of this stuff as soon as possible, I also know the risk of what can happen when things of this nature are done haphazardly. Remember an ounce of prevention can be worth a pound of smooth skin.

REPEAT WARNING: Cosmetic companies cannot use **ANY** form of Retin-A in their products. They will try to tell you otherwise. They will insist that some other less irritating, nonprescription form of the Retin-A is hiding out in their ingredient listing. They may point to the ingredient listing and tell you that vitamin A is much like Retin-A. It is not and there is nothing else around anywhere that can substitute. Retin-A by prescription only is the Retin-A we are discussing.

Retin-A: The Story

The story of Retin-A is less dramatic than one might expect from a cream that research indicates possesses the ability to alter the appearance of sun-damaged skin and wrinkles. You might have thought that Retin-A was some ingenious mysterious compound developed in some secret lab in the Alps or Himalayas with an exotic rare tropical root as its active ingredient, which would be wonderfully romantic and make great copy but be totally untrue. It all started about 20 years ago in Philadelphia (a very exotic location) at the University of Pennsylvania with the guru of skin care himself, Dr. Albert M. Kligman.

Known for his bold, outspoken and authoritative dermatological research on acne and aging, Dr. Kligman had been successfully using a derivative of vitamin A, known as tretinoin (Retin-A) for his patients with acne. After a period of time his older patients began noticing a startling improvement in the appearance of their skin. Not only did their acne get better but the lines on their face began disappearing at the same time.

Dr. Kligman was at first skeptical. He assumed his patients were under some type of psychological illusion. Perhaps they were so happy and relieved when their skin cleared up that they simply perceived themselves as looking better and younger. That would hardly be a surprising emotional side effect of feeling good about your skin and appearance. But that was far from the case. Ten years later some types of wrinkles were still disappearing and at a noticeable rate at that. As Dr. Kligman states himself, "I wish I could say it was creative genius but it was just an accident."

Accident or not, an independent group of scientists and dermatologists finally decided to do an independent study to scientifically discover or disprove what all the clamor was over this acne-fighting pharmaceutical. Their research took place over a 16-week period with 30 real live patients. At the end of the research all 30 patients who completed the study showed statistically significant improvement on their skin that was treated with Retin-A. The only adverse reaction cited in this experiment was that 92% of the patients developed some degree of mild to severe dermatitis. The results of this landmark research were published in the *Journal of the American Medical Association;* it was then enthusiastically reported on all over the world. To say the least, the Ortho Division of Johnson and Johnson, which owns the patent on Retin-A, is one happy company and so are their stock holders.

What It Really Does

According to Dr. Kligman and these independent researchers, Retin-A changes the appearance of abnormal sun-damaged cells back to normal, it rebuilds the collagen supply of the skin, it increases the skin's cell turnover rate, it eliminates a proportionate amount of the skin's leathery texture, it reduces the fine lines and some of the coarse sun-induced lines on the face, it influences the production of blood vessels and it changes the yellow color of the skin back to pink. Well, no wonder everyone is so excited. The flaw in the ointment: It also causes an inordinate amount of irritation which can be mild to severe.

When the news broke, many dermatologists who normally wrote 20 prescriptions a month for Retin-A were writing about 200. Pharmacists all over the country could not keep Retin-A in stock, which is both good news and bad news. It's good news that people now have a fairly inexpensive way to deal with some forms of wrinkling on their face. The bad news is that most of these people are not aware of how to deal with the side effects of Retin-A. But, as I'm sure you were counting on, I have a few suggestions which I think will help. Some of this will sound like a repetition of the earlier sections on skin care, but better you should be bored for a few paragraphs than make a mistake that could have been easily avoided. The chances of you increasing your tolerance of the Retin-A will be pretty good if you adhere to the following ideas.

Before You Start

When you receive your prescription for Retin-A be sure you are getting one for the .05% cream base. Do not use the liquid or gel; it will prove to be too irritating to tolerate because they both contain alcohol. Also be sure to ask your doctor for a facial cortisone cream at the same time or go to the drugstore and purchase an over-the-counter hydrocortisone cream. This way you will already have it handy when the battle of the irritation begins.

Two weeks before you start using Retin-A STOP using all irritating skin-care products on the face. Do not use any creams that contain fragrance or coloring agents. Do not use any astringents, toners or fresheners whatsoever. Do not use any facial masks or topical antibiotics. Do not use bar soaps of any kind on the face. Do not use wash cloths, buff puffs or scrub products on the face, even the baking soda is off-limits for one week before you start using the Retin-A. (The exception to that would be if you wanted to use the baking soda only over the blemishes that pop up, being very careful not to overscrub.) The most important way for you to start protecting your face is to begin using the water-soluble cleanser, Cetaphil Lotion. Use the baking soda judiciously or not at all and, depending on how dry your skin is, you can start using either Neutroderm, Lubriderm or Eucerin Lotion.

After You Start

Once you start using the Retin-A you can expect irritation to develop within the first week of usage. The skin may begin to peel, develop dry, scaly patches and possibly burn and itch. If you find that these side effects are more than your skin can comfortably handle you may want to cut back your frequency of use. You can also try avoiding the irritation by starting your treatment with applications only two or three times a week, which would slowly build up your skin's tolerance. If that still proves too irritating you can mix half your nightly application of Retin-A with an equal amount of the Cetaphil Lotion before applying it to the face.

Using Retin-A under the eye area is considered to be a good idea because of the improvement that can be seen in this area. Do not expect it to change bags under the eye or sagging skin. Retin-A will only have a positive effect on the leathery lines and crepey skin of the eye area. If you want to use Retin-A on the skin around the eye area, which is very delicate skin, you will definitely want to consider diluting a small amount of the cream with the Cetaphil Lotion before applying to this area or applying it every other night to start. Talk to your dermatologist to see if he/she agrees with this method.

Another option for you would be to use the topical cortisone cream you got from your doctor, or the nonprescription hydrocortisone cream you picked up at the drugstore, to help reduce the irritation. You would use either of the cortisone creams in the morning after washing your face with the Cetaphil Lotion, but before you put on your moisturizer. If your skin becomes very dry, the Eucerin cream can be reapplied two or three times a day. In conjunction with the Cetaphil

Lotion and a topical cortisone cream, this should alleviate most of the side effects as they show up.

You will be pleased to know that most of the irritation may stop after a few weeks or, in extreme situations, a few months depending on your skin's sensitivity. Your skin wants to do what the Retin-A is helping it do so it is only a matter of time before the skin adapts to the treatment.

WARNING: RETIN-A CAN MAKE THE FACE SUN SENSITIVE. That doesn't mean you can't go outside or play in the sun it just means that you need to be extra cautious about applying a strong sunscreen to protect the face. A 15 or greater block would be preferred. If you already have a tan, you can probably get away with an 8 but be careful. Bring both with and listen carefully to the skin. Retin-A keeps the skin in a constant state of peel, leaving the surface layer more vulnerable than usual. Be aware of this and act accordingly. It never hurts to check with your doctor to get his/her feedback before you do anything.

Smooth Sailing

If you do everything according to plan, the treatment procedure for Retin-A on sun-damaged skin should show noticeable results in about three to four months. Again, to assure this goes smoothly be certain you are starting with a low concentration of Retin-A, the 0.05% cream is preferred.

The suggested application is to use the Retin-A at night all by itself without a moisturizer, but if your skin requires a moisturizer to feel comfortable, don't hesitate to use one. In the morning, after cleansing the face, a moisturizer can then be applied as needed. Again, if irritation shows up you can change from using the Retin-A every night to every other night or diluting the amount you want to use with the Cetaphil Lotion and apply the cortisone cream over the irritated areas. Always be sure to check with your dermatologist first.

WHAT ABOUT WEARING MAKEUP? Good question, but I'm not so sure the answer is that good. For the first several weeks you will probably find it best to not wear much makeup at all, particularly foundation. I found that my flaking and peeling looked worse when I wore foundation. Eyeshadows and blush will also go on choppy over dry, irritated skin. Wearing moisturizer might help but it still may look like rough skin under there. For a month or two you should have no problems wearing mascara, lipstick, and eyeliner. For me after six weeks of using Retin-A my makeup started to go on smoother, but there were still some dry patches that looked more dry and flaky with makeup on, especially under the eyes. This is one arena you will have to test for yourself. The only thing you will definitely need to change is if you normally wear an oil-free foundation switch to a water-based foundation. Everything else should stay the same.

WHAT SHOULD YOU NOTICE? To sum up some of the things I mentioned earlier about what Retin-A does it seems that the following takes place once treatment begins: Retin-A thins the surface (epidermis) layer of skin by increasing cell turnover and stimulating the production of normal cells that often become abnormal as we age. This thinning of the surface layer of skin eliminates the thick leathery appearance of sun-damaged wrinkling and returns a pink glow to the face as a result of this increased cell activity. On a deeper level, in the dermis, the Retin-A appears to increase the production of collagen thereby thickening the support layers of skin which firms and plumps the tissue making the face appear smoother. Retin-A also stimulates the production of capillaries increasing the skin's circulation, which also brings a pink or healthier glow to the face.

How Long Is The Treatment?

According to Dr. Kligman, you can start using Retin-A and a sunscreen as soon as you can (or want to) and for as long as you can (or want to). His feelings are, that because of what Retin-A does to the skin, you can be on it for the rest of your life if you were so inclined. After about a year of regular applications he feels that a maintenance program of less frequent use can be continued which, according to his own research, should sustain the desired results of smoother skin indefinitely. Dr. Kligman suggests after you have used Retin-A regularly for a year or more you can use it for three to four months and then stop usage altogether for a period of six to nine months when you would then start using the Retin-A again for another three to four months.

Dr. Kligman warns that entirely discontinuing use can return the skin to its original condition. Skin seems to be pre-programmed to age and unless you stop using your face, going outside or tell the skin to do things differently with the Retin-A, your skin will grow up on schedule once the Retin-A therapy is stopped. The independent study was not quite as generous in their long-term forecast, but then again they only observed their patients for 16 weeks; Dr. Kligman has been doing this for 20 years. In the long run, what you choose to do is up to you.

NOTE: Not all physicians will be as generous as Dr. Kligman is about the claims that Retin-A can reduce sun-damaged wrinkles. However most all of the dermatologists I interviewed agreed that the positive changes in the surface layer of skin caused by Retin-A make it a worthwhile product. In fact many of the doctors I talked to used Retin-A themselves on a regular basis.

SUMMARY: 1. One to two weeks before you begin applying Retin-A stop using all forms of soaps, alcohol-based products, wash cloths, scrub products including the baking soda, moisturizers that contain fragrance, facial treatments, facial masks including my recommendation of the milk of magnesia and extended periods of time in saunas or Jacuzzis.

2. Twice a day wash your face with the Cetaphil Lotion and massage only blemishes very gently with the baking soda.

Do not massage the baking soda over the areas of your face where only blackheads are a problem.

3. Start applying Retin-A 0.05% cream base in the evening over the whole face including the area under the eye. Do not use your moisturizer at the same time if you can avoid doing so comfortably.

4. In the morning wash your face with the Cetaphil Lotion and then apply your moisturizer.

5. By the third or fourth day you may notice dryness and dry patches. Your face may also feel unusually sensitive and slightly itchy. The sides of your nose and the sides of your mouth may be particularly troublesome. You will want to avoid applying the cream directly to these areas. But remember this irritation will most likely disappear in a few weeks or less.

6. If the irritation and dryness is causing you problems you may want to cut down your applications to every other night or to three times a week. Keep in mind though that every night is preferable to see the desired results sooner. You can also dilute your nightly application by mixing half of what you would normally use with the Cetaphil Lotion and then applying that mixture to the face.

7. To combat the irritation you may want to apply a cortisone cream, either prescription or nonprescription, in the morning to those areas that are driving you crazy.

8. To combat the dryness you may want to try using Eucerin Lotion as your moisturizer in the morning or, if absolutely necessary, at night too.

9. You can apply makeup as you normally would. The only exception to that would be if you were using a foundation base that contained alcohol or was specifically labeled as being oil-free. When using Retin-A the only way you will find relief from dryness is to supply the skin with a little bit of oil.

10. Try not to scratch or rub the skin no matter how much it itches.

11. If you have any questions consult your dermatologist. There is also a consumer hotline provided by the Ortho division of Johnson and Johnson (the people who make Retin-A). You can call them collect at (201) 218-6504. For doctors and nurses who have questions their toll-free number is (800) 526-3979. Be aware that they will encourage you to use their products in conjunction with the Retin-A but they will have answers to other practical questions that involve use and not skin care.

What Happened To Me

Day 1 — Spent $30 for a rather large tube of Retin-A 0.05% cream base. I was told this would be about a three to four month supply. I have been very good about not using the baking soda all over my face. I only used the baking soda and 3% hydrogen peroxide where a blemish showed up. I also purchased a tube of cortisone cream that was safe to use on the face. I applied the Retin-A as directed and went to bed. The first night went by relatively uneventfully.

Day 2 — Excitedly I called my friend Julie to tell her nothing had happened but I was looking forward with anticipation to the next few weeks. The second night went pretty much like the first night.

Day 3 — I woke up with a tiny rash on my forehead. I also had several breakouts on my chin and cheek. My skin had a noticeable pinkness to it, like I had been out in the sun for an hour or so. My face also had a noticeable tingling sensation all over. After I washed my face with the Cetaphil Lotion I massaged the blemishes with baking soda. When my face was rinsed and dried I applied the cortisone cream to the rash on my forehead. That night I applied the Retin-A as I had before and went to bed.

Day 6 — Boy do my eyes itch and the sides of my lips are cracked and dry. Actually my whole face feels slightly itchy. The breakouts and rash on my forehead have disappeared and I've stopped using the baking soda and 3% hydrogen peroxide altogether. I've used the cortisone cream over the sides of my nose and at the corners of my mouth. There is a slight amount of dryness on my cheeks but nothing to complain about. Because I have naturally oily skin and a tendency to breakout I have not found it necessary yet to use a moisturizer. Before I went to bed I once again put on the Retin-A, trying to keep my hands off my itchy face.

Day 10 — The irritation seems not to be so bad this morning. Though the sides of my lips are still dry and cracked and my eyes still feel itchy. There is also flaking dry skin all over my face. My husband has started staring closely at my face saying, "You're paying someone to do this to your skin?" I hope at the end of the month we both will notice a difference. I'm going to be patient and see this thing through till the end of the tube.

Day 14 — I called Julie again today to tell her that my face is feeling much less irritated and itchy, my eyes aren't driving me crazy, the peeling on my cheeks has calmed down and the cracks on the side of my lips are better too. I have only been applying the cortisone cream every other day to the sides of my nose and the corners of my lips. I have used the baking soda two or three times, in the morning only, very gently, all over my face to help remove some of the scaling, but that was it. I haven't had any breakouts to speak of, and my face has a nice pinkness all over. All in all though, I'm remaining skeptical. I'm not going to get my hopes up, I'm just going to enjoy my skin's semi-return to normality and see if it lasts.

Day 16 — Julie called me. She wanted to know how things were going. She also said most of her friends were curious too. I reported in and said I was pleased with what was happening to my face but still apprehensive. I told her that I was noticing a change in the few whiteheads I have that never seem to go away. These small hard white lumps that don't do anything on the face but sit there seem to be breaking up. If they really do dissolve and go away that would be wonderful.

Day 18 — My skin is definitely doing better. My forehead is a little itchy but I will put some cortisone cream on and I'm sure it will go away quickly. My eyes hardly itch at all and the sides of my lips aren't cracked anymore. I stopped applying cortisone cream to those areas a few days ago. My skin feels a little tight and there is some dryness but not bad. I'm concerned about what will happen when my menstrual cycle shows up here in the next few days, but I'm hoping for the best.

Later That Day Of The 18th — A friend called to tell me that her hairdresser told her that there have been reports of Retin-A causing some people to bleed right through their skin! I asked where he heard that from, she said he just heard it. I said he should stick to cutting hair and stay away from medical assessments. Retin-A in the 20 years that it has been used as an acne treatment has never produced such an effect. Nor has any other research documented such absurdity. If the skin became that irritated, like the sides of my mouth did, perhaps a little bleeding may occur from the cracked skin, but then a cortisone cream needs to be applied or, as I explained earlier, you would need to cut back your frequency of application or dilute the application with the Cetaphil Lotion. But spontaneous bleeding is not possible.

Day 20 — Except for a general sensation of tenderness all over my face and a bit of dryness on my cheeks everything seems to be back to normal. Some of those whiteheads I was hoping would go away are much less noticeable. My skin still has a pink color that looks very healthy. There seems to be no difference in the lines on my face but then again I don't have many lines anyway. I still seem to have my share of breakouts which I deal with as they pop up.

Day 24 — My period came relatively uneventfully. I still had my usual share of menstrual acne but nothing a little baking soda and 3% peroxide couldn't handle. My eyes have been a little more sensitive than normal but it isn't all that uncomfortable.

Day 31 — The sides of my lips are dry again so I used the cortisone cream to help alleviate the irritation. My forehead seems to be more sensitive to the Retin-A than any other part of my face. I don't want to overuse the cortisone cream so I am cutting back my Retin-A application on my forehead to every other night.

Day 40 — I'm surprised how good my face feels. Other than the routine of applying Retin-A every night and using the baking soda only when I need it everything seems to be as it should be. I do notice a difference in the surface texture of my skin; it feels smoother, even when I'm breaking out it feels somehow softer.

Day 43 — *I went to bed late and forgot to use the Retin-A. I guess I'm becoming more relaxed about the whole experience.*

Day 47 — *It is warm in Seattle and I went for a bike ride with my husband being sure to apply a strong sunscreen before we went. I also packed some with me in case we were gone for a while and I would need to reapply the sunscreen to maintain protection.*

Day 49 — *My skin started flaking like crazy. It could be that the little bit of sun exposure I got the other day affected my skin. I gently used the baking soda all over my face and it seems to have taken care of it. By the way, a few days ago I stopped using the Retin-A on my forehead altogether. I still seem to get a rash every time I do and I'm not willing to continue reapplying the cortisone cream that frequently. Cortisone creams, with constant use, can negate any positive effects of the Retin-A.*

Day 55 — *I've been a little lazier than usual and skipped a couple of nights. I put the Retin-A on in the morning instead and everything seemed to go smoothly. I find that my face is much less sensitive than it has been since I started this whole process but it seems that my face still has its share of breakouts.*

Day 72 — *What I have learned after almost 3 months of usage is that Retin-A is indeed an experience. I have decided to continue regular daily applications for the next nine months and will probably continue with a maintenance program of twice a week after that. Unless the medical journals report otherwise I'm convinced that Retin-A is beneficial for the skin. My face feels smoother and looks it too. Not a startling change, I didn't have many wrinkles when I started, but enough to keep me interested.*

Questions And Answers — Clearing The Rumors

Q. I've heard that not all women can use Retin-A? A. That's probably true but I'm not sure who that would apply to. Perhaps someone with severe dermatitis, some other skin malady or extreme sensitivity would perhaps be the type who should avoid usage. But in those situations the dermatologist would be the one who could determine the advantages and disadvantages of Retin-A therapy. Other than that, Retin-A has such minor long-term side effects that it is essentially harmless to use, uncomfortable yes, but not harmful.

Q. I've read that the irritation caused by the Retin-A is so bad that it actually hurts the skin? A. It depends what you mean by hurt. Some people will react more severely than others to Retin-A therapy and in those cases it would be best to stop usage and consult your dermatologist. But if you mean permanently hurt, that is most unlikely. In the 20 years that Retin-A has been used as a prescription for acne there has been no permanent damage documented. The discomfort that is caused from the irritating side effects will eventually stop with continued applications in about two weeks to a month or two depending on your skin.

Q. When I got my prescription for Retin-A my doctor told me to continue using the skin-care routine I had been using in the past. Do you think that's a good idea? A. Depending on the skin-care routine I think it can be a great idea or totally rotten idea. If you are washing your face twice a day with the Cetaphil Lotion or some other nonfragranced, nonalcoholic, soap-free cleanser and massaging occasional blemishes with a little baking soda that would be perfect. But if you're using scrub products, toners, wash cloths, soaps, fragranced moisturizers, facial masks, steaming the face and the like, it is a sure-fire way to guarantee that your skin will over-react to the Retin-A. Much of the irritation can be avoided if you follow the skin-care routine I've outlined for the weeks before you begin and while you're using the Retin-A.

Q. I received a tube of Retin-A from a friend. Is it safe to use it without seeing a doctor first? A. It is probably safe but not very smart. Retin-A truly has little to no serious side effects that could not be eliminated if you simply stopped usage. What isn't smart, especially if you want to achieve positive results, is that if your skin does react severely to the treatment, you may quickly need a prescription for cortisone cream to reduce the initial irritation that accompanies the first applications. The other problem is that Retin-A comes in a few different strengths and bases; you will want to be sure you are using the one that is least likely to cause irritation. And finally, it is a drug and because all skins are different it wouldn't hurt to check yours out with a doctor before you begin treatment.

Q. How old do I have to be to start using Retin-A? A. That depends on what you want. Retin-A performs a number of functions that have benefits for all people who go out in the sun or are in the process of growing up. But in terms of seeing noticeable results that will demonstrate a difference in the texture of your skin, probably around the age of 35 or older is a good time to start. Remember, once you start using Retin-A on a regular basis for a year, you do not have to continue daily usage for the rest of your life. After the initial year you could go on a maintenance program that can be handled a couple of ways. You could cut your applications to three times a week or you could use the Retin-A for three to four months out of every year and the rest of the time just follow your normal non-irritating skin-care routine.

Q. I've heard that Retin-A is expensive, is it? A. Whether or not something is perceived as expensive is always a relative question. What seems overpriced to you may not be for me and vice versa. In my opinion, though, Retin-A couldn't be cheaper. The cost can vary but it averages out to around $30.00 for a large tube that should last you for three to four months and possibly six months.

Q. What about wearing makeup? A. Makeup should be no problem unless of course your face is having a severe reaction to the Retin-A. There are no inherent complications in wearing both; if everything is going smoothly, you could even wear the Retin-A under your makeup. Assuming of course that the makeup you're using doesn't contain alcohol or any other drying ingredients go ahead and do what you usually do. If your foundation is oil-free find another one that is water-based. If your face is going through a phase of irritation and dryness, and you haven't found any relief from the nonprescription or prescription cortisone cream and the Eucerin Lotion, then you will have problems wearing makeup comfortably. This period of skin sensitivity should go away. In the meantime you may want to consider wearing your moisturizer with only mascara and lipstick. Your face will let you know when you can start putting the rest on smoothly.

Q. Is Retin-A really an anti-wrinkle cream? A. The safest and most accurate answer to your question, as far as we know, is that Retin-A is probably an effective anti-sun-damaged wrinkle cream and an anti-cell-aging cream. What Retin-A does for the skin is reverse some of those processes that happen to the skin from sitting in the sun. It also reverses some of those processes that happen to the cell as we get older. Whether or not that visibly changes your wrinkles is something only you will be able to tell. What it will do regardless of a change in your wrinkles is change the surface appearance of your skin to a more healthy status.

Q. What if I don't usually sit in the sun, will Retin-A make a difference on my skin? A. Sitting in the sun is only part of the way your skin gets hit by the sun. Walking outside is the other part. The only people we know of who don't do either are Buddhist monks in Japan. These men, whose religious beliefs keep them inside in a meditative, expressionless and quiet lifestyle, at the age of 80 do not have wrinkles. For the rest of us who drive to work, walk to the park, laugh, cry, kiss and talk — we use the face and sun enough that using Retin-A could make a positive difference.

Skin-Care-Guide Summary:

1. Twice a day wash with a water-soluble cleanser. The one I suggest is Cetaphil Lotion, which is available in most drugstores. **AVOID BAR SOAP** and wipe off makeup removers. The water-soluble cleanser will remove your eye makeup at the same time you wash your face. Use tepid water — hot water burns and irritates, cold water shocks and irritates. Do not rub the skin dry. Gently blot the face dry with a soft towel.

2. If you have blemishes or areas where you break out, while the face is wet, massage blemishes with baking soda. Rinse well. Dry face gently. BE CAREFUL, you can overdue the baking soda.

3. Twice a day soak blemishes with 3% hydrogen peroxide soaked on a cotton ball. Let dry. Avoid the hairline and the eyebrow area with the 3% peroxide; the hair will lighten with repeated exposure.

4. For blemishes, as a facial mask, use plain milk of magnesia. It acts as a disinfectant and absorbs oil. But if you're not breaking out, if you don't have blackheads, then you don't need to use the 3% hydrogen peroxide or milk of magnesia. If you do have dry skin and still break out, use the baking soda, 3% peroxide and milk of magnesia over the lesions only.

5. If your skin is dry, moisturize by spraying the face with a light mist of water spreading the moisturizer over the water, let it absorb and, if needed dab off the excess. Do not rub or massage anything into your skin. The best moisturizer to use when out in the sun is one that contains a sunscreen. As of March 1980, any lotion containing 5% or more solution of sunscreen can be labeled as follows: "This product reduces the carcinogenic effects of the sun and retards premature aging." USE A SUNSCREEN AND REAPPLY WHEN SITTING OUT FOR MORE THAN TWO OR THREE HOURS AND IM-MEDIATELY AFTER SWIMMING AND EXERCISING.

6. At night, after your moisturizer has absorbed, pure lanolin, pure vitamin E oil or any pure oil can be used over drier areas instead of expensive eye creams, which generally contain the same ingredients. Read your ingredient labels.

7. Never use alcohol on your face. That includes all astringents, toners and fresheners. Alcohol's effect on the skin is dehydrating and irritating.

8. Remember that gravity plays a large part in the aging process. Don't help gravity do its job of pulling at the skin by wiping off your makeup.

9. See your dermatologist if you're curious to try Accutane for acne or Retin-A for acne and/or sun-damaged skin.

10. Be sure to never sleep with your makeup on. Makeup left on overnight becomes an irritant to the face. Swollen eyes, blackheads, dry patches and rash-like looking breakouts can often be traced to leaving makeup on for longer than necessary. Give your face a break and let your face breathe, your pores will be thankful you did.

There it is. Even if you're skeptical, my skin-care routine is so inexpensive it's worth giving it a chance. I've been doing it now for over nine years and my skin clears up when I just think of all the money I've saved.

A Few Quick Comments: Comparison Shopping

If you do venture out to find a cleanser (or any cosmetic) on your own, which I encourage wholeheartedly, here are a few shopping tips to keep in mind: Be aware that companies claim differences between products that often don't exist. At face value they may indeed look different but inside they can be quite similar. Comparing labels will help you find out if that's the case. In comparing water-soluble cleansers, if oil is listed in the first five-to-seven ingredients you can be sure it will be tricky to rinse off without the aid of a washcloth. Natural ingredients, medically tested or scientifically formulated cleansers as I explained earlier *sound* like they're good but those terms are all essentially meaningless. None of those things on the label reflect results, which brings me to the most important cosmetic advice I can render: Bottom line is that you need to try the product before you buy it. You can usually convince most cosmetic salespeople to give you a small sample if you supply the container. A container can be anything from a piece of tinfoil to a plastic baggy. Then at your leisure you can take it home and see if it works for you.

Speaking Of Ingredients

What can I say, the subject of ingredients is a book all by itself and one that will either bore you or confuse you beyond the point of sanity. Cosmetic chemistry is a complicated, highly technical field of study. To impart some of that knowledge is not an easy task, especially if I want you to stay awake for the rest of the book. What may be helpful to you is listing a few rules and suggestions about how to understand the only part of the cosmetic packaging that has any real meaning at all. I will explain specific chemical information in the appropriate section. The following list is true of all ingredient labeling regardless of the specifics about a particular ingredient or product.

1. Ingredient listings are legally controlled by the Federal Drug Administration.

2. Every cosmetic and pharmaceutical must have a list that includes every ingredient that is in the product. If the ingredient listing is not on the container itself, it will be on the package it came in.

3. Even if you do not understand the names of the ingredients (and who does besides chemists anyway) you can still become familiar with some of the basics that are in practically every product. Moreover there are many cosmetic ingredients that are far from mysterious, like: water, mineral oil, petrolatum, beeswax, vegetable oils, lanolin, glycerin, collagen, plant and food names, talc, fragrance and coloring agents.

4. Ingredients are listed in descending order. The first ingredient is the most abundant (probably 70% or more of the product's content) and the last is the least (probably less than .5% of the product content).

5. Long ingredient listings concern me. The more complicated the listing, the more likely that all those ingredients are not in there. Because of the FDA regulation that all ingredients be listed, cosmetic companies cover their bases by including what *may* be in their product. This way, if they run out of one ingredient or they have too much of another, they can change things around instead of holding up production. In addition the more ingredients the more things your skin has a chance to react to. Simple listings are more impressive to me than long ones.

Allergic Reactions

As I stated earlier, there is no such thing as a hypoallergenic cosmetic. It's a scientific-sounding word with no legal basis. The same is true for Allergy Tested products. Though the products may have indeed been allergy tested, it doesn't tell you which allergies were tested or on whom these tests were performed. Dealing with allergic reactions to cosmetics takes more information than those useless phrases and terms could ever provide. Many allergic reactions are caused from a combination of products: Your foundation mixed with an eyeshadow, or a moisturizer worn under a new blush. It isn't always one particular item that could be causing you problems and to make matters more complicated, emotions can play a major part in what is making your skin react. Your moisturizer and the fight you had with your husband could trigger a skin reaction. The next week, the same moisturizer, minus the argument, may reveal no reaction. There is also an additional stumbling block that makes allergies a very frustrating experience: What you are not allergic to today, you may become allergic to tomorrow and vice versa.

One of the most common irritants in a cosmetic is the fragrance. Fragrance-free moisturizers are a wonderful way to avoid those problems. But if your skin is not that sensitive or allergic to cosmetics you do not have to be that careful with the fragrance in your makeup items. Other allergens are some of the irritants I've been referring to all along: alcohol, scrubs, soaps, and natural ingredients like herbs and vitamins. Avoiding those potential problems is relatively easy.

As I briefly mentioned earlier, a typical allergic reaction can come from falling asleep while still wearing your makeup. Makeup left on overnight can be a powerful irritant to the surface of the skin. Next time you wake up in the morning with half your makeup on and half your makeup on the pillow, it won't be such a mystery what caused your eyes to swell and itch or your face to breakout.

If you are convinced that you did have an allergic reaction to a product return it. Most companies will refund your money. Cosmetic companies need to be informed of products that may be causing problems for the population as a whole. If you don't inform them they won't know.

Beyond allergic reactions there are severe reactions or complications that do occur because of problems with cosmetics. Do not be afraid to take care of whatever happens by consulting with your physician or going to a hospital emergency room. It is not your fault and your health is very important.

Drug vs. Cosmetic?

Federal legislation distinguishes a drug as: "articles for use in the diagnosis, cure, mitigation, treatment or province of disease or intended to affect or change a structure of the body." Cosmetics are described as: "articles for use intended to be applied to the body for cleaning, beautifying, promoting attractiveness or improving the appearance." In this country, drugs are strictly controlled; cosmetics by comparison have little to no controlled guidelines at all.

The reason you may want to know the difference between cosmetics and drugs is because there is a big difference as to how much research a cosmetic has to go through before it comes to market and how much research a drug needs before it can be sold to the public. Cosmetics require NO proof that they can do what they claim they do. A drug requires years of expensive substantiated research before it can be released for mass-market sales. Cosmetic claims often sound borderline like a drug, but as long as it is a cosmetic there is no research needed to backup any of the things the label declares.

In all fairness that legal difference in a few situations works against the cosmetic companies. For example, many cosmetic companies use effective sunscreens in their products but they don't label the product with an SPF number. Once they do that the product would become a drug and require all that expensive testing I was just talking about. For the most part the cosmetic companies take advantage of the lack of cosmetic regulations required by the FDA, but the sunscreen area is not one of those.

Hair Removal

Hair, whether it be on your head or any other part of the human anatomy, can pose problems. On the head it's usually the problem of not having enough and on the body it's usually having too much. Excess body hair can be taken care of in one of five ways: shaving, tweezing, waxing, bleaching (lightening the hair) and electrolysis.

Shaving is inexpensive, easy and great for large areas like the legs. For women, shaving the face is a mistake that is often hard to stop once you get started. After shaving, grow-back inevitably begins in less than eight hours and a 5 o'clock shadow or stubble on any woman is never desirable.

Tweezing is great for small areas like eyebrows, but for larger areas it is time consuming and because of variable hair growth, can be a painful everyday procedure with no end in sight.

Waxing is much like tweezing in that the hair is being yanked out close to the root. The difference is speed, waxing is fast and it gets lots of hair all at once. Unfortunately, the grow-back for waxing and tweezing is about the same. The negative part of waxing is that you have to wait for the hair to grow back in and obtain some length before you can wax again.

Bleaching is excellent for small areas and I prefer it to waxing and tweezing for facial hair. There is no grow-back or stubble, it's inexpensive and can be repeated as often as needed. The negative about bleaching facial hair is that many of the specially made products available on the market turn the hair yellow and yellow facial hair is not necessarily that much better than black. A good bleach recipe you can use to turn the hair completely white is the following:

1 Teaspoon Lady Clairol Instant Whip

2 Teaspoons Clairoxide Developer (20 volume peroxide)

5 Pinches Lady Clairol Lightening Booster
(comes in a small red and white package)

Mix together and let stand for one minute. Then apply to hair with a cotton swab. Wait ten minutes and then rinse off with cool water.

Electrolysis is wonderful for truly unwanted hair that won't change with fashion like moustaches and chin hairs. The problem with electrolysis is that it's expensive, time consuming and, depending on the technician who performs the procedure, it can be a total waste of time and painful. Be sure to check out the credentials and obtain personal recommendations if you opt for this procedure.

Liposomes

I wasn't going to include this section on liposomes but then, at the very last minute, just before I sent this book off to the printer's, I pulled the pages from the waste basket and included it anyway. My reluctance to write about this was because there aren't many products on the market that contain liposomes, so it may be difficult to find. To make matters worse, even those products that claim they contain liposomes often use a version of this ingredient that is ineffective and there's no way you could tell that from reading the label. In spite of those concerns, because liposomes are a fascinating ingredient that can do interesting things for dry skin, I decided to share what I know.

A liposome is a cosmetic ingredient that is used in moisturizers. Once applied to the skin it works much like a timed release vitamin or hayfever pill. Timed-release medications allow you to take one pill that lasts over a long period of time. Once swallowed the chemicals are slowly released into the bloodstream. This way the capsule's entire contents aren't dumped into the body all at once, where it would be used up quickly requiring you to take more in order to sustain the pill's benefits. Now imagine that time-released effect waiting for you inside a moisturizer.

What normally happens when you put on a moisturizer is that each ingredient has a particular destiny: Some of the mineral oil spreads **over** the surface of the skin and some of the vegetable or animal oils are absorbed **into** the skin. A very small amount of the water spreads over the surface of the face and an even smaller portion of that is absorbed into the skin. (Most of the water in a moisturizer is never absorbed into the skin because it is absorbed by the air before it has a chance to go anywhere else.) The water that is absorbed into the skin and the water already in the cell will only stay there for as long as the oil stays around. As anyone with dry skin will attest to, that isn't all that long. The mineral oil on the surface of the skin is easily wiped away and the vegetable or animal oils are eventually completely absorbed. The effects derived from wearing a moisturizer only last as long as the moisturizer is present. *But*, if your moisturizer contained liposomes that scenario would be completely different.

For lack of wanting to describe the involved molecular structure of liposomes, what I would like to explain is what they do once they are applied to the skin. Much like a time released capsule, liposomes allow the moisturizer's oils and water to stay in place until released by the action of the liposome breaking down when it is absorbed by the skin cell. It works something like this: Imagine that a liposome has two or more hands. With one of these hands it grabs an oil molecule and in the other hand it grabs a water molecule. The liposome, still holding hands with the water and oil, is absorbed together with them into the skin. Once inside, these little friendly groups line up around the skin cell. When one of the liposome groups gets next to the cell it will be absorbed, which will release the oil and water to do their job of moisturizing the cell.

Get the picture? After several applications of a moisturizer that contains liposomes, billions of these hand-holding water and oil liposome groups are lined up around the skin cells waiting their turn to be absorbed. That means even after you wash your face, you can't wash away this kind of moisturizing process because it is taking place in the skin and not on the surface. Isn't that a fascinating process?

The only product I know of that contains the type of liposome that really does this timed-release action is a product called Candermyl. It is hopefully available in your local drugstore. Ask your pharmacist if they have heard of it. If they haven't, they can order it from Dermatological Products of Texas. If you choose to try other liposome type products on the market, you will know within a few days if it works. If you have very dry skin you will notice a dramatic difference, especially on your hands. After you wash your hands with soap they should not feel dry like they usually do. The need to run to a moisturizer to prevent painful dry skin will no

longer be there. You will need to reapply, but there won't be
the urgency.

Skin Care On Television

Every now and then, when I happen to be flipping through
the television channels, at the strangest times I run into these
half-hour-long, paid-for television commercials about skin care.
They seem to carry on endlessly about a new, wonderful, three
or four step answer to your skin-care problems. These lengthy,
misleading, hokey, insulting skin-care ads are the most blatant
testimonials to the very things I hate most about the way the
cosmetic industry sells products to women.

I have listened with my teeth clenched as the inventor
and interviewer carried on about how their thousands of clients
love the products, love the inventor and love their skin's
healthy glowing appearance. These painfully loving claims go
on with occasional cutaways of how your skin can find happiness too if you send for these miracles today. Of course at no
time does anyone discuss what the ingredients are, who the
manufacturer is, how long the products have been around,
how they compare to other like products on the market, or
what to do if you have an allergic reaction.

I cannot stop these commercials from airing or prevent
you from wasting your money. But I can tell you to consider
the amount of informationless dribble you're being handed
and ask if you want to use products that are being sold in
such an overly hyped manner. Remember, without useful information you can never make a consumer-aware decision.

Chapter Six

Assessing Who You Are And How That Affects Your Makeup

A Personality & Image Profile Test

The reason I've chosen these tests to introduce the makeup chapter is because I feel strongly that they will help you with the process of evaluating what kind of makeup look you could be wearing. The answers will help you discover what style of makeup is best suited for you and how your personality can help or hinder your ability to adapt that look. Personality traits are the way we interact with the world. Image is how we want to be seen. Making those two work together in harmony will hopefully be easier when you've finished this chapter.

The first test I want you to try is the type that assesses what kind of personality you have. Management seminars love having you take these personality tests for two reasons: The first one is because they are very entertaining. The second one is because they quickly and objectively allow you to assess how your personality reacts to different situations and problems. Perhaps you've taken a few of them yourself. The general format of these personality profiles is to have you answer a set of questions that describe certain emotional characteristics and traits. For example, given the following set of words you would be asked to select the ones that fit you best: Sensitive, Independent, Sociable, Bold, Diplomatic, Scheduled, Adaptable, Spontaneous. You would then be grouped into a category corresponding to your responses. If all went well the group of adjectives you chose would most likely describe your primary personality type.

Even though I love tests it basically goes against my nature to want to put myself or other people in categories. I don't want to think of myself or anyone else as being just like all the other people who happened to select the same answers I did. Yet, regardless of this hesitation, I still find this kind of test fascinating for the simple reason that no matter how many times I've taken different personality profiles they always hold true for me and they also always seem to hold true for everyone else in the room who was taking the test with me at the time. Without fail I fall into the same group every time and what they describe about that group always sounds like they've known me all of my life.

Of course there are grey areas where the test is not perfect. I remember one test I took, where I thought for sure I belonged in another category. The facilitator assured me I was in the right group. He suggested that I did have some of those other personality traits but rather it was the style in which I operated that placed me in the group I found myself. There are always parts of you that have cultivated aspects of the other personality groups but it is always the *way* you approach life that defines who you are and the primary group you belong to. I'll explain all that more clearly in a moment.

For the personality profile there are only two questions you have to answer. Here they are:

Question 1 — On a 0-to-10 scale, with 0 being the least, rate how **formal** or **informal** you see yourself. You cannot score a 5, you have to be either a 6 and above or 4 and below. 10 means you are a very formal person and 0 means you are a very informal person.

Before you choose a number keep in mind that formality has nothing to do with how casual you are. You can be casual and formal at the same time. Consider the following scenario to judge your formality quotient. For example, very informal people who *throw* a casual party may serve potato chips by tearing the bag open and leaving it on the somewhat cluttered sofa table for people to help themselves. The keg of beer and the soft drinks would be in the refrigerator with the overflow sitting on the floor waiting for room to be made as the supply diminishes. Also, the mismatched glasses or paper cups left in their wrapper would be on the counter along with the paper plates and the roll of paper towels to be used as napkins.

Very formal people never throw a casual party — they give or host a get-together. They may also serve potato chips, but the chips would be placed in a bowl and set on the dining room table that has been cleaned for the occasion. They would serve beer, but most likely it wouldn't be a keg, unless it was a keg of Coors or Heineken. The glasses, which may or may not match, would be properly chilled. Paper plates and paper towels can still be the choice for serving, but they would be set out in a neat arrangement along with the plastic cutlery. Get the picture?

Another example would be the way very formal people might dress to a casual party. They would wear freshly pressed jeans or loose-fitting neatly creased slacks with a matching sweater and T-shirt underneath. Their shoes would be almost new or at least polished and would match the general feel of their outfit.

The way very informal people might dress for a casual party would be to first look through the laundry to find the slacks they forgot to wash. The shirt they didn't iron will probably not match the color of the slacks, and their sweater will possibly have a hole or torn seam somewhere.

How formal or informal you are has nothing to do with money or education, it is simply how you approach and organize your life. After considering the previous descriptions give yourself a formality rating between 0 and 10, with 10 being the most formal, being sure not to use 5 as a possible score.

Question 2 — On a 0-to-10 scale, 0 being the least and 10 being the most, rate how **passive** or **assertive** you see yourself. Again, scoring yourself as a 5 is not an option, you must choose a 4 and below or 6 and above. This question tends to be a little easier to judge in yourself than the first one, but because it is so easy, you may want to ask a few people who

GRAPH A   Formal

```
                              10

                               9

         X-------------------X8
         :
         :                    7
         :
A        :                    6                              P
s        X                                                   a
s       10   9   8   7   6    5   4   3   2   1   0           s
e                                                 X          s
r                             4                   :          i
t                                                 :          v
i                            3X-------------X               e
v
e                             2

                              1

                              0
```

                    Informal

know you well to help you with the answer. Ask them how they see you in terms of assertiveness or passiveness and have them give you a score. Balance their answers against your initial reaction and choose the number that best fits you.

Here are some ideas to help guide you: If you were a very passive person, given the option of asking someone to do something for you or doing it yourself, you would probably do it yourself. On the other hand, you would have a rough time saying no to someone if they were to ask you to do something for them. Also, a very passive person would find it difficult to understand why anyone would place emphasis on schedules or doing things quickly and exactly.

Very assertive people always delegate responsibilities to other people and never hesitate asking for help. The only time very assertive people don't ask for help is when they think no one else could do it better than they can. Very assertive people know when to say no, and understand the need for doing things properly and quickly. Get the picture? Now on a 0-to-10 scale, 0 being the least assertive and 10 being the most assertive, rate yourself being sure not to use 5 as a possible score.

Take your two numbers and, finding the question they match, place them on graph A.

Now plot your points on the graph by drawing lines from each score to where the two intersect. This intersection puts you in a particular quadrant on the graph and as you may have already guessed, each quadrant represents a particular personality style. Check graph B to find the name of your section.

GRAPH B

Controller	Analyzer

Enthusiast	Supporter

The Results

The Controller category is where my scores always place me regardless of what the test questions may be. If you scored in this group we share many things in common. We like to be in charge. No matter what it is, we want to take control of what's going on. Whether you're an executive, a salesperson or a housewife, you want to get the job done now and you want it done right. And if the job can't be done now you want to know when. Controllers have homes that are as formal and organized as they are. The main strengths for this group are getting things done, getting them done efficiently and getting them done beautifully. Thank goodness for Controllers because without them how would we ever get anything completed.

The Controllers' weaknesses interestingly enough turn out to be the fallout of their strengths. We tend to compulsively need to get things done so we have trouble relaxing. We also tend to not let anyone else relax either. We're known for being stubborn, tenacious and no matter what anyone else says, we're right most of the time. Flexibility is not a word you would associate with the high-scoring, formal and assertive group of Controllers.

The opposite end of the spectrum, diagonal to the Controllers, are the Supporters. This amiable group is known for being easygoing and relaxed. Their laid-back attitude in life is highlighted by their desire to help people. If there is a group to join, Save The Whales to Save The Local Grocery Store, Supporters are there to sign up. Not that Controllers don't join groups that save things, it's just that when they do join, they take charge, implement new policies and tell the Supporters what to do. Supporters have homes that are known for their comfort, their lives are comfortable, their clothes are comfortable and their general outlook on life is comfortable. They love life and if life needs a helping hand they're there to help out. Thank goodness for Supporters because without them who would ever lend a helping hand?

Much like the Controllers, the Supporters' weaknesses are a direct result of their strengths. In essence, Supporters have never really learned to say no, or if they do say no they can't make it stick, which means they never get a chance to do what they want because they're always busy doing what other people want. Supporters are also so comfortable they tend to be out of sync with the rest of the world's pace. If they need something they want it without too much commotion or hassle. The beat of the drummer they hear is always playing a slow, easy waltz and they wonder why everyone else isn't taking the time to listen.

The group adjacent to the Supporters are the Enthusiasts. Even though these two groups are side by side on the graph, their differences make them worlds apart. Enthusiasts are full of energy and life. They love new ideas, exciting people, parties, more ideas, events, more parties and more ideas. They are constantly creating excitement and drama wherever they go, and they are on the go all the time. If there is someone who is the life of the office or the party, or if there is someone who always has a story, it's the people in this group. Enthusiasts also join groups that save things, but they join every group and start a few dozen more of their own. Thank goodness for Enthusiasts because without them where would all the creativity and joyous energy in the world be?

Enthusiasts aren't going to recognize their weaknesses; that's because they are too happy and excited about things to believe they have any. How could anyone who is so happy have weaknesses? Therein lies their flaws. Their energy is so frenetic that it is hard to pin an enthusiast down. If they get you interested in one idea, the next time they see you it will have been forgotten and another dozen will have taken its place. Enthusiasts tend to be flighty and unreliable because of their need for constant stimulation. This group can be so busy and yet so undisciplined that they never stay with any one thing long enough to get any one thing completely done.

The Analyzer group is my favorite because without them there would be no charts, no scores, no tallies and no data anywhere in the world. We would also not have this section of the book either. They are the scientists, engineers, accountants, bookkeepers and detail gatherers of the world. They love taking notes and keeping track of things. Their biggest joy is research. They are information mongers. Libraries are a source of pleasure for Analyzers, and they wouldn't leave home without their calculators. They understand the pros and cons of a situation or dilemma better than any of us, because you can be sure they have accumulated all the necessary information to make their list complete. Analyzers also join groups that save things and when they do they keep all the records in order and up to date. Thank goodness for the Analyzers because they help us know the reality of things and keep us informed of the facts.

The Analyzers know their weaknesses because they have figured them out long ago. They understand that the incessant need to gather information makes it hard to make a final decision. If you are constantly in need of more research and data, it is almost impossible to ever stop and say, "Let's do it this way now." Analyzers tend to say, "Let's get more information." Their rigidness makes them a little hard to reach. They find it hard to let their hair down, though if they did, they would know for how long, what the temperature was and whether or not the benefits the next morning were worth it.

Personality and Makeup

How does each personality group choose which makeup design to apply? Each group has a specific personality style: This style coincides with an attitude about how that group would generally like to be seen by the rest of the world and how willing they are to adapt their appearance for the sake of fashion and career. Let's look at the Controllers as a first example. They are the most formal of the four groups and they are the most formal about their makeup. They tend to wear the most makeup, but whether they wear a little or a lot they want it to look fashionable and they want it to match what they're wearing. Controllers understand the place makeup has in their "dress for success" look. The idea of outfitting the face is a term they fully comprehend. On the other hand, there are Controllers whose desire to be fashionable is blocked by their need to be right. This attitude often prevents them from seeing themselves objectively. They have trouble doing things differently once they've done anything for a while. After all how can they be wrong? The only way to impress change upon Controllers is to let them know that it will help them be more effective in life and waste less time.

Supporters generally don't like wearing makeup. Besides being too formal and too much trouble for them, they are uncomfortable with the way it feels and the way it makes them appear. Besides, Supporters don't understand all the fuss about fashion, much less makeup. This group is the hardest to reach with makeup ideas because it really isn't part of their personality to be that concerned with the exterior, which at times, I feel is an enviable trait. Perhaps balance is the key to strive for?

Enthusiasts love wearing makeup but they tend to always go a little overboard. They either wear too much color or too severe a design. Or, if it isn't the amount of makeup that's a problem it's the time it takes to do a good job. The time it takes to develop good reliable makeup habits is too tedious for the energies of an Enthusiast, so their makeup tends to look a little messy and disorganized. The other thing about Enthusiasts is their willingness to try something new. Unfortunately, they are *always* trying something new so their makeup look tends to be eternally eclectic. The only way an Enthusiast will consider a less random approach to makeup is to see how exciting life could be if they had a more sophisticated appearance.

Analyzers like wearing makeup as long as it is simple and goes on precisely. What they don't want is to make a fuss and they don't like to be in the limelight. What they do want is to wear the bare minimum and do it tastefully and carefully. You can always recognize an Analyzer's makeup: A nice lipstick color, one soft eyeshadow on the lid and a little blush will be neatly in place. Analyzers are the easiest group to show an efficient and effective makeup routine to because they can relate to anything that is efficient and effective. They love change when it is logical and when it works.

How We Handle Change

There is a lot to be gained from looking at how we deal with what life hands us and how that establishes why we dress or wear our makeup the way we do. As you read the information in the makeup chapter about the pros and cons of different cosmetic products keep in mind that the way you react to that information may be more influenced by your personality than the information itself.

For example, at one point I discuss the alternative ways to line the eye. There are pencils, liquid liners and powder eyeshadows that can be used as liners. Each of those options has its own merits and problems. Depending on your personality you may lean more toward one or the other. Supporters will NOT want to wear any eyeliner no matter what, Controllers will want to wear the eyeliner they're already wearing, Analyzers will want to wear what is the easiest and goes on the softest and the Enthusiasts will want to wear what is new and exciting. All of those attitudes are the way those personality groups might usually respond. The alternative for each might be as follows:

The Supporter may want to consider how a more dynamic makeup look may help them appear more assertive to the rest of the world. The Controller can consider the notion that what they were doing worked in the past, but there may be another option that is just as fashionable and perhaps more workable. The Enthusiast may want to slow down and decide to take a more reliable approach to their makeup and give up their previous eclectic approach. The Analyzer simply needs enough information in order to do things differently, and hopefully I've done my job and provided what she needs.

Dress Your Face According To Your Image

The second part of this self-analysis is to take a look at the external image you want to project in your business and personal life. This image profile involves reviewing a list of six basic characteristics and then choosing the one that best describes how you want to be seen in the world. After you've completed this section you can possibly approach how you get dressed every morning in a more concrete, goal-oriented frame of reference. The confusion or the steadfastness that sometimes accompanies how we choose to put ourselves together every day can be solved once we let go of our self-image stubbornness and just deal positively with what we want. This test isn't about right or wrong, it is only a way to help you get what you want.

The same hesitation I have with the personality profile test I also have with the image profile test — a resistance to being categorized. But again, for the most part, the system works as a logical tool to get you headed in the right direction, or if you are already headed in the right direction it can reinforce what you already know.

Your personality is a separate issue from the image you want to project in life. The words that are associated with image are radically different from the words associated with the personality types we discussed in the previous section. Personality is the automatic attitude you use to approach life with and the internal style you rely on when dealing with issues. Image is the external appearance that, like a book, tells someone who you are in the world. If you can project that image in harmony with your personality strengths, the road to success will become much more accessible to you. Some women spend a great deal of time confused about who they want to be. Once you end the struggle of how you want to be seen, who you want to be just may fall into place.

To take this test simply read each image characteristic list. Once you've finished, go over the list and select the description that best describes how you want to be seen in the world. If more than one applies, that's okay; I'll explain how that all can work together when you're done. The professions that are listed in the image profile list are not meant to be used as a career guide. Rather you can use them as a way to evaluate your present look. For example, if you are employed or looking for employment as a Management Specialist and you are dressing more like the ARTIST you may want to reconsider the image you've chosen for yourself — your appearance may be working against you and not for you.

Image Characteristics

Image 1 — THE ARTIST

PROFILE: The Artist is an image of one who is daring, creative and dramatic and wants to be recognized as such. New ideas that run the gamut from art to literature fuel the fire that keeps the Artist alive.

PROFESSIONS: Graphic Artist, Writer, Novelist, Entertainer, Publicity Manager, Columnist, Actress, Dancer, Dance Instructor, Choreographer, Drama Coach, Art Teacher, Director . . .

CLOTHING: To create this image in clothing, hemlines and silhouettes are far less important to you than adventurous, new wave color combinations, fabric textures and jewelry. Unexpected and yet fashionable, unique though not out of place, is the look that depicts the Artist.

WARNING: The risk with this image is the chance that you might get too carried away and look strange instead of interesting, particularly if you're employed in a more conservative job. A traditional business suit can appear more *arty* by adding an exotic scarf or hand-crafted earrings for accessories.

MAKEUP: Makeup holds the same potential hazards for the Artist as does her wardrobe. Too much color and over-dramatic eye makeup can change the look of an up-and-coming Artist to a beatnik who never grew up.

Image 2 — THE PROFESSIONAL

PROFILE: No matter what else the Professional is doing her true focus is geared toward either advancing her career or trying to create one. The Professional is happiest when she is being productive and effective.

PROFESSIONS: Any position within the corporate world that allows room for advancement or any entrepreneurial venture that provides room for expansion.

CLOTHING: Dress for success or power dressing is the rule of thumb for this image. Slightly exaggerated shoulders, nylons with a simple elegant design and diamond earrings are a few options that always look like success.

WARNING: This is a look that can become a uniform if you let that happen. A man's suit is for men, not you. Don't lose yourself in the corporate image. Use your personality profile to help you gauge how casual, formal or frivolous you can be within the boundaries of your professional look.

MAKEUP: Makeup for the Professional tends to be problematic because too much can be just as bad as too little. The Professional, in order to be taken seriously, needs to find a full makeup look that is a happy medium both for herself and the image she wants to project.

Image 3 — THE ATHLETE

PROFILE: The Athlete puts incredible import in being strong, moving easily without hindrance and enjoying the feeling of being healthy. In everything the Athlete does, whether it is work or play, the desire is to always be seen as one who is physically capable of accomplishing anything and everything.

PROFESSIONS: Nutritionist, Health Administrator, Aerobics Instructor, Gym Teacher, Forester, Recreational Specialist, Occupational Therapist or Specialist, Athletic Trainer . . .

CLOTHING: Wearing clothing that is restrictive, too slick or too fashionable will feel awkward on you and out of place. The preppy look with oversized tweed jackets, denim or corduroy well-tailored skirts with simple leather flats can make this statement nicely without compromising fashion or femininity.

WARNING: The Athlete needs to be careful about being perceived as being too masculine. The fear of ruffles and frilliness often pushes the Athlete too far in the other direction, and there is a happy medium to be found.

MAKEUP: Makeup can help the Athlete from appearing too masculine, but balance is essential. Too much color, too much mascara, or too much lipstick can look out of place. The rule here is tasteful simplicity. Athletes can easily get away with the minimum amount of makeup, but the minimum needs to be noticeable.

Image 4 — THE TREND SETTER

PROFILE: Simply stated the Trend Setter knows what's going on, and you can tell by looking at her that her information is up to date and accurate.

PROFESSIONS: Fashion Consultant, Specialty Sales, Public Relations, Advertising Sales, Attorney, Insurance Sales, Stock Broker, Clothes Buyer, Interior Designer . . .

CLOTHING: To make this statement clearly and concisely, your clothes should be either classic so that you're never out of style, or the most recent fashion selections from the European and American designers' seasonal offerings. If the latter is your preference, you will need to spend a lot of time at the better fashion stores in town so you always have the latest fashion look in your closet.

WARNING: The Trend Setter can prove to be one of the more expensive images to create and maintain for yourself; also be cautious about being so up to date that you look out of place.

MAKEUP: Your makeup can pose the same conflict as your wardrobe. If you are always choosing colors that are up to date, you have to live at the makeup counter, incessantly in the process of trying something different. I would always vote for a classic look just to be on the safe side while you're building this cutting-edge, trend-setting image.

Image 5 — THE EDUCATOR

PROFILE: The Educator is the look that epitomizes knowledge and the essence of what being a communicator is all about. The classroom is not the only forum for this well-informed image; business consultants and professional speakers often love donning this appearance.

PROFESSIONS: Teacher, Company Trainer, Product Specialist, Systems Implementation, Author of How To Books, Accountant, Sociologist, Education Development, Printer, Acquisitions Editor . . .

CLOTHING: Elegant glasses are the classic accessory that depicts this image, but the best way to convey this statement is with tailored business suits in strong colors, or neutral business suits with vibrant-colored blouses. Conservative with a flair to be noticed and heard is the dominant theme here.

WARNING: The Educator is a cross between the Professional and the Artist, which means you can run the risk of appearing too boring if you stick to a business suit or too overdone if you try to compensate too creatively with accessories and colors. Balance is essential for the Educator.

MAKEUP: Your makeup should be the same blend as your wardrobe; conservative is the best approach with a vibrant lipstick or dramatic eyeshadow thrown in for attention.

Image 6 — THE DIPLOMAT

PROFILE: The Diplomat is the peacemaker in the world, the one that handles disputes and is always looking for the perfect compromise. Negotiating is a skill that comes second nature to the Diplomat.

PROFESSIONS: Politician, Public Relations, Housewife, Personnel Manager, Secretary, Retail Sales, Doctor, Nurse, Counselor, Lobbyist, Office Manager, Caterer . . .

CLOTHING: The wardrobe that best portrays this image is a soft business look. Two-piece suits with formal fabric are fine, but the silhouette should be unstructured. Or you can wear the exact opposite — a tailored business suit made out of casual fabric. Colors should be subdued so as not to offend anyone and the patterns can be subtle and beautiful.

MAKEUP: Your makeup should reflect the same statement as your clothing. A full makeup look represents confidence and respect, but the colors should be soft and subtle to avoid distractions.

Image Theory

What do you do with the image you've chosen? **BE THE WAY YOU WANT TO BE NOW.** This is a philosophy I truly believe in because I've seen it work for others and it has worked for me. Years before I ever conceived the idea of owning a business, being a reporter or writing books, I made the decision that how I looked wasn't the way I wanted to be in the world. I knew back then that I wanted to look sophisticated and worldly. I also knew I wanted to be noticed. No matter what I did in the world I knew those *images* were important to me. According to this list of image characteristics I wanted to be a cross between a Trend Setter and a Professional. Back then the only image statement I was making was — struggling college graduate, can't afford much but trying anyway. Not a self-assured image by any stretch of the imagination.

Slow but sure I started to invest in myself. I still didn't know what I wanted to do in the world, I only knew how I wanted to be perceived. I took pictures of outfits I admired in fashion magazines and went to discount stores to try and put them together for myself. I did the same with my makeup. I bought a book by the famous photographer Scavullo and tried to copy the makeup applications I saw in there that matched how I wanted to look. With time the new me began to emerge and I began getting the reactions from people I wanted. The more confidently I dressed, the more confident I acted and the more confidence people put in me. This, in essence, is the concept behind finding out what image you want to project and starting to make it happen.

NOTE: I hear some of you saying you can't afford to do this. That stumbling block doesn't apply here because money isn't an issue in this goal. How *much* you own isn't what makes image happen. No matter how much you spend or own, if it doesn't say what you want it to say about you, you've wasted your money. Most everyone buys some amount of clothes or makeup some of the time. Now when you shop the idea is to shop with a purpose, keeping how you want to be perceived foremost in your mind all of the time.

Putting The Two Tests Together

The way to begin is to keep your personality type in mind so you don't let your weaknesses get in the way of the image you want to project. The second step is to find an image that feels comfortable and go for it, allowing nothing to stop you. Together these are the tools that can help you take an objective look at how you presently do things and how you can do them differently. Here are a few examples:

For me, I fall into the Controller personality group and I want to project the image of the Trend Setter mixed with the business savvy of the Professional. My personality type works well with both of the images I want to project, except that my pocketbook dictates that I stick with classic looks rather than the latest fashions. Traditional styled suits with padded shoulders and conservative patterns, worn with brightly colored oversized silk blouses, work well for me. My makeup is always classic and I let my lipstick color vary with the tone of the blouse I'm wearing. I feel that the Controller part of me can be too formal and stiff so nowadays when I go shopping for makeup or clothes, I try to cultivate the Enthusiast part of my personality by trying a few more daring, artistic items than I would normally be used to buying.

My friend Christina is the true Artist and a strong Controller. Her bold choice of clothing styles, color combinations and textures is always exciting to me. Wisely, her makeup tends toward the conservative, which serves as a nice balance so Christina never seems to appear too far out or extreme.

A woman I used to work with was someone who saw herself as the consummate Professional with overtones of the Trend Setter who was also an Analyzer's Analyzer. She was one tough IBM Corporate Executive. Letting her hair down meant putting on a pair of freshly dry-cleaned jeans, full makeup and two-inch heels instead of three. She dressed for success even when she was gardening. Her image was overtaking her. If this woman had taken these tests, she could then use the Analyzer part of herself to take an overall assessment of her image. Then she might be able to notice that her life was out of balance and lacked variety and freedom. Maybe she could have recognized that letting go of her formality once in a while or developing a more casual style that fit her formal framework would have been a viable option.

Stephanie is a body builder who works as a Dental Hygienist. She loves her work and loves her body. After taking this test she spotted herself immediately — she was a Supporter who wanted to always be seen as an Athlete. True to form she was concerned about looking too masculine or too formal but felt awkward about wearing most of the styles she saw her female patients wearing. After taking this test she recognized that her tendency was to be afraid of makeup and clothes in general. She found both to be restrictive. Stephanie had never considered a preppy casual look as an option for herself. Her Supporter personality was worried about not being comfortable, and the Athletic image she loved kept her from dressing the part of herself that was vibrant and interesting. Recently, Stephanie has bought a few wonderful casual sweaters that she matched with a beautiful tweed skirt and oversized corduroy slacks. She has also started wearing mascara, lipstick and blush; not too much, just enough so that you know it's there.

Now it's your turn. After each section that describes a particular makeup technique or theory, you can evaluate your reaction or need to learn that step by looking back at the explanations of the groups you *fell* into and chose for yourself. Then at the end of the makeup chapter, I will sum up the makeup options that I think work best for each personality type and each image selection.

Chapter Seven

A New Beginning For You
And Your Makeup

A Quick But Honest Introduction

The way I introduced this chapter in the first book was by writing the following: "It has never been recorded in history books that anyone has ever dropped dead from modern makeup." Well, that's not altogether true. Back in the 1800s both men and women, in the name of fashion, used powder makeup bases that contained lead. The result of this deadly fashion *Glamour Don't* was that many *attractive* people literally died from lead poisoning. Since those days we have come a long way and our skin can face makeup with relative worry-free use. What I should have said, that I will take the opportunity to say now, is that it has not been recorded in the annals of modern medicine that women are dropping off like flies from using and wearing makeup. In all fairness to the cosmetic industry, the colors and varieties of products they produce are generally wonderful, easy to use and last a reasonable length of time. They also do not melt in the hot sun or freeze during the winter when left in a makeup bag inside a car while you go shopping, do not grow strange molds or fungus despite the fact that most cosmetics will spend most of their lives in a hot damp bathroom, and the side effects of wearing makeup produces little risk of permanent damage to the skin or eyes. So what do I have to complain about if all of that is true? Funny you should ask!

Someone asked me once, why, if I was so upset with the cosmetic industry, didn't I just stop wearing makeup. That would be like asking Ralph Nader, if he was so angry with the car industry, why didn't he just stop driving a car and walk. Being angry with some aspects of the car industry doesn't necessarily mean Mr. Nader doesn't like to drive to get where he's going. He may, in fact, love to drive. It's just that while he's behind the wheel he wants to be assured that he's getting his money's worth of quality and safety. Makeup for me is the same thing. I enjoy the remarkable effects that can be created with makeup, but that doesn't mean I want to buy over-priced makeup which smears, flakes off and is accompanied with over-inflated claims. I only want to deal realistically with the products I buy to put on my face, nothing more and nothing less. And that is exactly the kind of information you will receive in the next two chapters.

I love being creative with makeup, but I will neither deny nor overstate the wonders and problems of what putting the stuff on is all about. The intention will be to list in a very straightforward, matter-of-fact line of reasoning, the pros and cons of wearing each type of cosmetic item it takes to accomplish a fashionable makeup look. I will also explain why some products aren't worth bothering with at all. Once you know the positives and negatives, you will find making decisions about what to wear and how to wear it easier and less costly.

With that in mind, this next section explains the makeup application techniques and theories I have developed over the years. Having applied more than a few lipsticks that bleed all over the place and mascaras that make lashes brittle and spiked-looking, or foundations that have gone on heavy and streaky, I have just a few opinions as to what I have found works and doesn't work. As a makeup artist, TV commentator and a woman who definitely enjoys wearing the stuff, my priorities are to be sure my makeup looks attractive without wasting time to achieve that appearance. That step-by-step formula is what I am about to describe in detail.

Before You Start

Because makeup goes on poorly over unclean skin, it goes without saying — even though it's been said a million times before — the first step in proper makeup application is to start with a clean face. More often than not, after washing your face with a water-soluble cleanser you can start applying your makeup. (This is one of those suggestions I was mentioning that you may have resistance to.) The only time I recommend using a moisturizer under makeup is when the skin is very dry. If your skin is not exceedingly dry, you are following the skin-care routine I outlined earlier and you are using a water-based foundation, a moisturizer is a waste of time and can actually lessen your chances of your makeup lasting all day.

I know that sounds radical, but in the long run it makes the most sense. Most water-based foundations contain the exact same ingredients as your moisturizer does, so it isn't necessary to double up products. By wearing a moisturizer and a water-based foundation at the same time your face can become too greasy and the rest of your makeup will tend to slide right off never having a chance to make it past lunch. If you feel a moisturizer helps your foundation go on smoother, there could be a problem in your application technique or the type of foundation you're using, which will be discussed in the section on foundations.

You may have also been told that wearing a moisturizer will *protect* your skin from the foundation and that is simply not possible. It's a good selling gimmick but miles away from the truth. Moisturizers are made to absorb into the skin and once they do, for all intents and purposes, they're gone and they can't prevent anything else you put on from going where it wants. Whatever layer of protective moisturizer might be left on the surface of the skin would be wiped away as you applied your foundation.

SUMMARY: My first theory of makeup application — **NEVER DO MORE THAN YOU HAVE TO!** Wearing a moisturizer under a water-based foundation, for most skin types, can be a waste of time, money and lessen the chances of your makeup staying in place throughout the day. When your skin feels dry no matter what you do or becomes drier as the day goes by choosing to wear a moisturizer is a good idea. If that is what happens to you then Lubriderm is as good a moisturizer as any to use before you start applying makeup.

Never Do More Than You Have To!

Speaking of doubling up products, special eyelid foundations, blemish covers and color correctors that are meant to change your skin tone are completely unnecessary. They complicate an otherwise simple process of applying makeup by adding more products than needed, requiring additional blending and forcing too many colors to interact on the skin at the same time. Your foundation can quite nicely accomplish all the functions those extra products are supposedly designed to handle without any of the fuss and expense.

Special Eyelid Foundations are sold to the consumer because they are meant to help eyeshadows stay in place longer. If we believe that line of reasoning shouldn't we expect to need a special cheek foundation to keep our blush on longer? The truth is eyelid foundations are usually very similar to regular face foundations. These two so-called *different products* can be almost the same thing packaged in different containers. Placing your face foundation on the eyelid will perform the same function the special eyelid foundation was supposed to accomplish, especially if you do not wear a moisturizer underneath.

Blemish Coverups are sold to the consumer solely because of something I call acne anxiety. The hope that is conveyed by the name *coverup* is that this product really can hide a blemish, and nothing could be further from reality. Most coverups are a heavier texture than your foundation and over a blemish that will appear thick and obvious. Or if the blemish coverup doesn't match the foundation exactly it will look like a different layer of color placed over a blemish bringing more attention to the very problem you were trying to hide. If the coverup turns out to be the same color as your foundation you will still end up placing too much extra makeup over the lesion.

Your foundation all by itself is more than sufficient to do the job of covering the redness.

The idea of covering up blemishes is a tricky problem separate from the products they've designed to do the job. Acne anxiety at times makes us do weird things to our faces. We scratch and pick at our faces, causing unsightly scabs that we then try to cover over with makeup. What we end up with looks more like an obvious mess than something no one was supposed to notice in the first place. Leave your face alone except for the suggestions I've outlined in the skin-care chapter and understand that covering up is something you can only do with a blanket and not a specialized makeup product.

Color Correctors are those bottles of pink, lavender or yellow liquid that are meant to be worn under your foundation to alter skin color. These little gems are hard to find anymore, but some cosmetic lines are steadfast in making you believe you need them. The notion is that if your skin is pink or ruddy in color you need to tone that down with a yellow tinted color corrector. If your skin is olive or sallow in color you would use the pink color corrector to change that. Interesting concept, but totally a waste of time, and, as the products are presently formulated, they can't do what they say they can do anyway.

The ingredient listing on most color correctors is very similar to moisturizers, which means they easily absorb into the skin. Once absorbed, you are supposedly left with a slight tint on the surface of the face that has changed the tone of your skin. In actuality, once the liquid has absorbed the effect is so minor as to have no effect at all. For the sake of argument though let's say there is a noticeable effect. The color of the corrector tint on your skin would mix with your foundation and you would end up with a very strange shade of foundation. The initial premise is actually faulty from the beginning. I do not believe that pink skin needs to be yellow and yellow skin needs to be more pink. That kind of thinking is what destroys feminine self-esteem every time.

SUMMARY: It's hard for me to imagine that anyone believes they need or want to wear a moisturizer, color corrector, eyelid foundation, blemish coverup and foundation just to get the face ready for blush and eyeshadows! Remember makeup Theory 1 — **NEVER DO MORE THAN YOU HAVE TO**.

Highlighting — Making Dark Look Light

I bet you thought I'd never get to the part where you would finally be able to start putting some form of color on your face. Your patience has been appreciated. It is interesting to note that the first two steps in actually applying makeup color are to reduce the darkness under the eye, and then apply a foundation to even out the skin. Once that is done, the eyeshadows and blushes can blend on smoothly over an even palette instead of varying degrees of skin textures and colors. Whether you start your application with the highlighter or the foundation depends on the color of the highlighter you use. For the sake of organization, I'll start with the highlighter.

The need for a highlighter under the eye is to offset the natural shadows that occur because of the way the eye is set into the skull. This shadow is often compounded by the skin's tendency to be extra dark under the eye. The first thing you will need then is a white or extremely light fleshtone highlighter.

The logic for using a white or nearly white fleshtone color is because of the same basic rule you learned in *Art 101*. When you need to make a can of paint a lighter color, you use white or as near to white as you can get. Any other color would defeat the purpose. Blue, yellow or regular shades of skin tone, like your foundation color, would be useless to gain the effect of making something dark lighter. When shopping for an effective highlighter be sure you keep your eye on the lookout for the very lightest shade possible or you will find yourself still looking at dark circles under your eyes.

The other consideration to keep in mind is that the high-lighter is meant to blend with your foundation so that no edges or abrupt lines of demarcation can be seen. If you use a fleshtone highlighter it will mix with the color of your fleshtone foundation and you will simply end up with a third color under the eye which will not necessarily be any lighter, only different.

The way to choose which color highlighter to wear is to follow these next few suggestions: If the area under the eye is very dark a white highlighter would work best. If the under-eye is only slightly shadowed try using the lighter shades instead of plain white.

You would only use the white, near white, or very light fleshtone highlighter if the area under the eye isn't already light by itself. If the undereye area is naturally white, like a goggle effect, it may actually be necessary to apply a color that is slightly darker than fleshtone under the eye to reduce that mask-like separation.

If you want to lighten the undereye area when you are not wearing a foundation, choose a foundation color one or two shades lighter than your regular color to use alone under the eye. A lighter-colored foundation worn as a highlighter

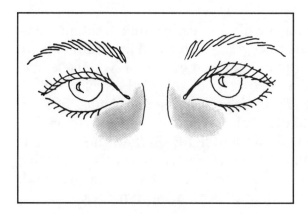

A) **CONCEALER**

Place white concealer on with the index finger or cotton swab hugging the inside corner of the un-dereye area.

under the eye should go on thin, but not too thin, without being obvious and still give enough coverage.

NOTE: If you've chosen to use a white highlighter, you would apply this highlighter first and then your foundation. If you have chosen to use a very light shade of highlighter, you would first apply your foundation, then the highlighter.

Types Of Highlighters

Highlighters come in basically three different forms. They are creams, sticks and liquids.

STICK HIGHLIGHTERS

Description: Stick highlighters come in tubes like lipsticks.

Application: They are applied to the undereye area much like a lipstick is applied to the mouth. They can be applied over or under your foundation.

Pros: Stick highlighters provide excellent coverage for very dark circles under the eye.

Cons: Stick highlighters tend to be dry and pull too much when you try to blend them in place. They also go on heavy and thick, which makes them difficult to blend unless you are wearing a moisturizer around the eye area, but that will only make the highlighter slip into the lines around the eye, looking caked and smeary.

LIQUID HIGHLIGHTERS

Descriptions: Liquids generally come in small squeeze containers.

Application: You would use your finger to transfer the liquid highlighter to the under area. Liquids go on thin and watery, which makes controlling placement tricky.

Pros: Liquid highlighters provide very light, next-to-nothing coverage.

Cons: Liquids have just the opposite problem of the stick highlighters; they have too much movement so they are hard to control. Also, because the liquid highlighter goes on in too thin a layer, it offers very little coverage.

CREAM HIGHLIGHTERS

Description: Cream highlighters come in a soft smooth form with a creamy firm texture.

Application: Cream highlighters go on easily with your finger or a Q-tip and blend evenly with most foundation types. You can place it either under or over the foundation.

Pros: They are usually the right consistency, not too greasy and not too dry, and they are hopefully a soft but substantial enough texture to give good coverage without appearing too thick or heavy under the eye. This type of cream highlighter should work well with almost any water-based foundation. In addition, because the product is a cream it tends to contain the same ingredients as a moisturizer so if your skin isn't dry it will still not be necessary to use a moisturizer around the eye area.

Cons: Unless the cream is too greasy or too dry, I can't think of a problem with choosing this type of highlighter.

CONCLUSIONS: The type of highlighter I strongly recommend are highlighters that come in a creamy cream form.

Placement: Placement is always the same regardless of color or the type of highlighter you use. Depending on the length of your nails (because when nails are long you can hurt yourself) use your finger or dampen a cotton swab to control the cotton fuzzies and place the cream highlighter in a half-inch crescent from the corner of the eye called the tear drop (see diagram) out to approximately 1/3 of the way under the eye. Avoid placing the highlighter all the way under the eye in a sweeping half circle. Placing the white all the way around the eye can create a goggle effect. Only place the highlighter on the eyelid when it is also dark and needs some lightening.

Blending: If you are using the white highlighter do not do any blending until the foundation is placed on the face. First the white goes on as described above, and then the foundation. After the foundation is smoothed into place, the last area you blend is the white highlighter together with the foundation under the eye, dabbing while you blend.

When using one of the lighter, nonwhite shades of highlighters, place it on in the same manner and place described above AFTER the foundation is blended all over the face and eye area. Once the nonwhite highlighter is in place over the foundation, carefully blend the two together in a dabbing motion.

Regardless of the color highlighter you choose, the foundation and highlighter are always blended together under the eye, being careful not to spread the highlighter onto the cheek or over the nose. The trick is to keep the highlighter blended only over the area where it is needed.

WARNING: As you may already know it is often recommended to use the highlighter over facial lines to make them less apparent. I think that whole process looks more obvious because of the extra layer of makeup it places over the lines. Highlighters can also be used over the center of the nose, top of the cheekbone, chin and other areas for accent and enhancement. All of those things are indeed options, but they are complicated and time consuming even for women adept at applying their makeup. Plus you can net the same results by applying the rest of the makeup correctly. I've used none of those techniques on my makeup as it appears on the cover and all those areas appear highlighted because of the way I've applied the rest of the makeup.

Foundation

Personally I've never been thrilled with the whole process of smearing foundation all over my face or even part of the face. So why do I recommend using foundation at all? Because of the glide most foundations create on the skin. If you try to blend your other blushes and shadows on without foundation the rest of the makeup will generally go on choppy. Foundation is also needed to keep those powdered colors in place. Since skin all by itself has no adhesive properties, foundation gives the rest of the makeup something to hold on to. Blushes and eyeshadows do have some ability to cling, but not much. Blushes and eyeshadows have more in common with baby powder than anything else. Ever put powder on after showering? Where does most of the powder end up? Right on the floor. Applying powder shadows and blushes will net the same result if a foundation isn't there to prevent them from falling off.

Blending: The best application tool to use when applying foundation is a flat, square or round, one-quarter-inch-thick sponge that doesn't have holes and is not made out of foam rubber. The shape and density of this kind of sponge provides the smoothest application possible. Using a cotton ball or cotton pads will deposit tiny pieces of cotton all over your face and when you try to blend with it, you end up wiping more foundation off than on. Fingers are also not a good choice to use when trying to blend foundation in place. Your fingers will streak and blend the makeup unevenly. Imagine the streaky appearance of finger painting; using your fingers on your face will result in the same appearance.

The sponges that you find most frequently for sale at cosmetic counters are the thick-wedged foam rubber sponges. These sponges are the most incredibly difficult things to use. They crumble after a few uses, are hard to wash, drag over the skin and, because they are so thick, most of the foundation absorbs into the sponge where you can't get to it, which can waste a lot of product. Wedge sponges are used primarily in the theater for a heavy greasestick foundation which needs to be pulled across the face in order to apply it evenly but that is the last thing you need when wearing a water-based, light-weight foundation.

Natural fluffy sponges that have holes (I'm not sure why they're called natural) will also cause problems when used for blending foundation because of their thickness, which absorbs too much foundation; the holes, which will leave empty patches on the face; and, because they aren't flat, it is almost impossible to get an even application. Imagine a paint brush shaped like this. Natural sponges are used in theater and T.V. for pancake type makeup, not everyday liquid foundations.

Even Application: Using your nice flat square sponge, shake some of the foundation from the bottle onto the sponge which you will then transfer to the face. You can use your fingers in the same manner but you will use only the sponge when you begin blending.

Placement: Start by placing the foundation generously over the CENTRAL area of the face, avoiding the sides of the face near the hairline, jaw and chin. The foundation goes on

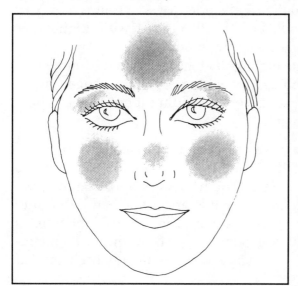

B) FOUNDATION
With a sponge, apply foundation generously to the central area of the face only, concentrating on the upper ⅔. Then blend with a dry sponge in a down and outward motion. Always avoid placing color near the jaw. Over the eye, fold sponge in half and dab foundation in place.

in large patches or dots over the white highlighter, nose, eyelids, cheeks and forehead but only in the center. Avoid placing lots of dots or patches of foundation all over the face, which can cause too much foundation to be blended into the hairline and the jaw where you need less foundation than you do in the center. (See diagram)

Holding the sponge between your first three fingers and thumb, spread the foundation down and out over the entire face, avoiding the eye area, in the direction of the hair growth with a stroking, buffing motion. The idea is to blend the foundation color from the center, where you initially placed it, into the perimeters of the face, leaving no line of demarcation at the jaw or hairline. Use the edge of the sponge without foundation to dab away any excess foundation that tends to collect under the eye. You can also use the sponge to wipe away any of the excess that gathers at the hair and jawline.

NOTE: When blending the foundation, do not try to force it *into* the skin. There is a fine line between blending something on and wiping something off. Instead, blend a thin layer over the face smoothing it with your sponge as you go.

Once the foundation is blended over the face and over the upper lid you should be left with a glob of white highlighter and foundation sitting patiently under the eye. Now you can finally blend the white highlighter together with the foundation under the eye by dabbing, not wiping, with the sponge. Saving the highlighter for last prevents blending it onto areas where you don't want it to go.

If you choose to use a very light fleshtone highlighter you would have to blend the foundation in place under the eye as well as the rest of the face. The next step would be to apply the fleshtone highlighter over this area and then dab it into place with your finger or sponge. The white highlighter is blended together with the foundation. The fleshtone highlighter is blended on after the foundation has already been applied and blended.

Watch Out For The Neck: Never ever put makeup of any kind on the neck. The foundation should match the skin so exactly that you only need to blend down to an inch or more above the jaw line to insure that a turn of the head doesn't rub makeup onto your collar. Makeup on collars is not where you ever want makeup to end up.

Double-Check Your Blending: There are places on the face you will be likely to miss with foundation that need to be checked. These are the corners of the nose, the tip of the nose, the corners of the eyes especially over the highlighter, and the edge along the lower eyelashes. There are also places that you will *hit* with the foundation that you should avoid. These are the ears, the jawline and the hairline, especially on blonde hairlines. Be careful to remove this excess if you've gone past your mark. Both problems can make your makeup application appear sloppy.

Keep Your Sponge Nearby: The sponge is a wonderful blending tool to keep near you at all times. When the edges of your blush or shadows need softening you can work with the side of the sponge that was used to spread the foundation over the face to blend out the hard edges. Using the side of the sponge that has foundation on it as opposed to the dry edge allows the sponge to glide over the blush instead of dragging, which can tend to streak the makeup.

Mini-application: If you hate the feel of foundation like I do, it isn't necessary to apply it all over the face. Remember, foundation is only needed to give the blush and shadows something to adhere to. When the foundation color matches the face exactly, and after you finish this section it will, you can apply a mini-application of foundation over those areas where the other colors will be placed. This way you won't feel heavily madeup and the blush and eyeshadows will still go on evenly.

To apply a mini-application start with the highlighter as you would for a full application, and then place the foundation only over a mask-like area between the eyes and mouth, including the nose and cheeks. There is no coverage needed on the chin, forehead or jaw area. Be sure to blend the edges carefully with your sponge.

Matching Skin Color

Keep in mind that skin and foundation should match exactly. If you are pale accept the fact that you are pale and buy a foundation that matches exactly. Do not buy a foundation that will make your face look a shade or two darker. Even that slight a difference runs the risk of being more obvious than you really want it to be.

I wish choosing a foundation wasn't all that complicated, but it is and that's because trying to explain how to match skin color is one of the more confusing aspects of makeup application. The crux of the problem is when you're told to match the foundation with your skin tone, exactly what is meant by skin tone?

Traditional names associated with skin color are: olive, when the skin appears ashen or green in color; sallow, when the skin takes on a yellow or golden shade; and ruddy, when the skin has overtones of pink or red. Unfortunately, this information can be misleading when it comes to choosing a foundation color. If your skin tone is ashen are you going to choose an ashen foundation? Or if your face is very pink are you going to buy a pink foundation? When purchasing a foundation whether your skin is olive, sallow or ruddy isn't what's important. What is important is to identify what your underlying *flesh* color happens to be. The actual overall flesh color of the skin is what you are looking for. For the most part, regardless of race, nationality or age, that means your skin, 99% of the time, is going to be some shade of yellow. Specifically, some shade of yellow-brown.

The coloring cells of the skin contain melanin, which is brown. The amount of melanin in your skin determines how brown you will be. The yellow color of the skin comes from the carotene in the skin. Carotene is the same substance you find in such foods as zucchini and carrots. In fact, if you eat enough foods containing carotene, your skin will take on a definite yellow cast. Therefore human beings are various shades of yellow-brown. What we are not are various shades of orange, pink and rose like you find in so many bottles of foundations.

The pink appearance in the skin can come from the tiny blood vessels found close to the surface of the skin called capillaries. How apparent these are on the face depends on your circulation, the thickness of the skin and the amount of melanin present. A pink-looking skin can also come from broken capillaries that look like tiny red lines on the face, sunburn, skin irritation and acne. Sallow skin means the face has little to no pinkness present, olive skin is similar with additional melanin present. For black skin the gold in the skin is oftentimes fairly obvious. Black skin can sometimes become ashen in color as the skin grows up; though the exact reason for this is not known, it is suggested that it could be a result of the skin becoming thicker.

Next time you purchase a foundation stay away from the pinks and rose tones that overcolor the face. I know that the idea of buying a yellow or yellow-beige or yellow-porcelain, or a pale tan color of foundation can sound like you'd be buying an unattractive foundation. The pink and rose tone foundations sound more like you would be smoothing on pink glowing skin, but believe me that is not the case. All you will be putting on is a foundation that will look very phony on your skin and be difficult to blend. The foundation is only the base that you then build the color design upon, and because of that it is essential for it to be fleshtone and not rose or pink. The color on the face is placed on selected areas when you apply the blush, eyeshadows and lipstick — and not all over the face with your foundation. Choose a realistic color foundation that might not sound pretty but will for certain give you the best results.

This same rule holds true for women of color; their skin needs to be matched with a golden shade of brown, chocolate or ebony-colored foundations that should all be yellow-based. The names of darker-colored foundations always sound beautiful so you will need to be extra careful not to be seduced into thinking that the name of the foundation will impart that color. In fact, even more so than for Caucasian foundations, black foundations for some reason seem to be orange in color. Do not make this mistake — a foundation called cinnamon might sound good, but you could be painting red tones on your skin when what you want is golden-brown.

An Exception To The Rule

Although in theory you are attempting to match your skin color exactly, in actuality you need to match the foundation to the neck. That's not as complicated as it may initially sound. If the face is darker than the neck and you put on a foundation that matches the face it will look like a mask because of the difference in color between the two. The opposite is also true. If the face is lighter than the neck and you put on a foundation that matches the face, it will still look like a mask because of the difference in color between these two areas that are so close to each other. This color difference doesn't happen often but it happens often enough so that some of you should know about it.

SUMMARY: The rule for foundation choice is that you should always try to match the yellow-brown color of the skin exactly, except when: **1. The face is lighter than the neck;** then it will be necessary to choose a foundation that is slightly darker than the face. **2. When the face is darker than the neck;** you will then need to use a foundation that slightly lightens the face. Always use your sponge to help blend any evidence of the foundation along the jawline.

Types of Foundation

Now that you know how to apply your foundation and which color foundation you need to buy, the last stone to look under is what type of foundation is best suited to your skin. There are five basic types of foundations: oil-free, water-based, oil-based, pancake and greasestick. Pancake, which is an oil-free type foundation, and greasestick, which looks and feels just like its name, are for theatrical purposes only. Pancake is a round tin of color that looks more like a face powder than a foundation. It turns into a foundation when it is rubbed with a wet sponge and is then applied to the face, drying quickly into place. Greasestick is heavy and thick in texture and is applied by using a small foam rubber sponge. These two foundations are not typically used on a regular basis by most women, thank goodness, so the focus will be on the other three types.

OIL-FREE FOUNDATION

Description: Oil-free makeup has absolutely no oil in it whatsoever. There are two forms this foundation comes in: One looks like a bottle of colored water that contains mostly talc, alcohol and coloring agents, the other looks like a traditional creamy, thick foundation which contains water, waxes, emulsifiers and coloring agents.

Application: Oil-free makeup that is creamy in texture, rather than watery, goes on like most other foundations — using the sponge as your blending tool. The differences appear after it is blended and dries quickly into place with a thick, solid finish that shows no reflection or shine.

Pros: The creamy oil-free foundation is a good foundation choice for photography and television work when you do not want the skin to shine at all. This is the type of foundation I wear for television appearances. It will also last much longer on oily skin than any other foundation type, which for some women is a very desirable effect.

Cons: The disadvantage of using the creamy type of oil-free foundation is the heavy mask-like appearance and feeling it creates when it dries on the skin. In order to get this makeup on evenly, you have to blend quickly or it will dry in place before you know it and then it won't budge unless you add water or wash it off. You have to get it on right the first time because once it's blended on it doesn't move. Adding water to your sponge to make it go on thinner tends to make this type of foundation streak. In terms of applying shadow and blush, this foundation is more difficult to work over. Because oil-free makeup has no movement (oil in a foundation allows for movement) the powders you use will have a tendency to stick to it, which can make blending difficult and correcting mistakes a nightmare.

Women of color or women with tan skin should avoid using an oil-free foundation, even if it's the right color for you, because it can look grey and ashen after it's applied to the face and dries. Skin that shows no shine or reflection in general can tend to look dull, grey and ghostly and with this kind of foundation that becomes even more true for women of color.

CONCLUSIONS: In spite of all these negatives, creamy oil-free foundations are a viable option for those who have oily skin, work in front of a camera and who know how to handle the negative side effects.

WARNING: Oil-free foundations that are watery in appearance contain mostly alcohol and should never be used. The alcohol content irritates the skin, increases oil production and dries out the skin at the same time — which are the very things you were hoping to avoid. They also go on poorly: After applying, when the water and alcohol evaporate, leaving the colored talc behind, the talc adheres to the skin unevenly and the chances for smooth coverage become impossible.

WATER-BASED FOUNDATIONS

Description: Water-based does NOT mean oil-free, it simply means that the first ingredient is water, and the second or third is usually oil. These foundations appear like a thick liquid and pour slowly out of the bottle.

Application: A water-based foundation if applied correctly should feel lightweight. In most cases it can go on in an even, thin layer. If you want heavy coverage you will probably be disappointed in a water-based foundation. When using the sponge to blend you will not need water to help your application because the foundation itself is already the right consistency.

Pros: Most water-based foundations are the perfect type to wear alone without the aid of a moisturizer. As I explained before, when the foundation and moisturizer contain many of the same ingredients, there is no need to wear both, and water-based foundations usually fit the bill. The oil part of this foundation gives it some amount of movement which allows blushes and eyeshadows to blend on effortlessly over the face and mistakes are easily buffed away with the sponge.

Cons: If you have very oily skin you will prefer using an oil-free foundation over the water-based type. The little bit of oil in a water-based foundation will show shine almost immediately if you have very oily skin. For those of you who do not have oily skin but have a paranoia about any shine on the face, you will also not prefer the effects of a water-based foundation; the small amount of oil in this cosmetic may make you nervous.

CONCLUSIONS: I personally don't feel there are any disadvantages to using water-based foundations and I recommend them wholeheartedly. Water-based foundations are also a good option for women of color. If you are concerned with the small amount of shine water-based foundations leave behind on the skin try using a light dusting of loose powder.

You can apply the powder all over the face after you've blended the foundation in place to reduce the glow and see if that works for you.

OIL-BASED FOUNDATIONS

Descriptions: Oil-based foundations have oil as their first ingredient and water usually as their second or third. Oil-based foundations feel greasy and thick, look greasy and thick and go on greasy and thick.

Application: Because of the tendency for oil-based foundations to be heavy you can help blend a thinner layer of foundation over the face by adding water to the sponge before you begin blending. If you wear face powder over this type of foundation the oil will grab the talc and the face can appear thick and heavily madeup. The same is true for blushes and eyeshadows — they will go on heavier because of the increased oil on the skin, and they will also become darker once applied.

Pros: It can be great for women with very, very dry skin who also want more coverage from their makeup.

Cons: Oil-based foundations are greasy, thick and heavy. They also have a tendency to turn orange on the skin because of the way the extra oil affects the pigment in the foundation. The oil will also grab any powder shadows or blush you apply to the skin, which can make the face look over-madeup.

CONCLUSIONS: The typical recommendation for using oil-based foundations is to add water to your sponge so that it goes on thinner, more like a water-based foundation. Why not just use a water-based foundation in the first place and skip the negatives of the oil-based foundation?

NOTE: For women of color, including those with dark tans, oil-based foundation can make your skin look orange after it is worn for a while.

SUMMARY: If what you want from your foundation is one that goes on easily, looks smooth and even, shows as few flaws as possible, gives the rest of the makeup something to adhere to without looking as though you're wearing a mask, then, if you haven't guessed by now, I am partial towards a water-based foundation. The pros definitely outweigh any negatives. The exception occurs when the skin is very oily, then the creamy type of oil-free foundation is good to use; not wonderful, but better than water-based.

Powdering

Description: Powdering the face, after you apply foundation, is optional and depends on your own personal preference. The need for powder is based on the amount of shine you want to reduce after you apply your makeup, or the shine that can build up as the day goes by.

Application: When you do powder the face, use loose translucent powder that is the SAME color as your foundation and apply it with a large, full, round brush. Pick up some of the powder on the full of the brush, knock out the excess and brush it on in the same motion and direction you did the foundation; that will keep everything going in the same direction and help retain a smooth appearance. Before powdering, use your sponge to buff away the excess oil from the face.

Pros: Powdering the face is an effective way to handle the oil shine that can make the skin look slippery and wet.

Cons: I personally do not like powdering immediately after applying makeup on myself or on someone else. I prefer some amount of reflection on the skin. To me, that represents healthy, glowing, alive skin. Skin that shows no sign of reflection looks dull and dry. I know there are levels between looking dry and looking like an oil slick, but you can handle that by NOT using a moisturizer under your foundation and blending your foundation on in a thin layer with the sponge. The amount of shine you get from the foundation alone should look like perfect, glowing, moist skin. As the day goes by, if you need to touch up your makeup, that would be the perfect time to use a light dusting of loose powder over the face.

WARNING: When you do use powder do not use pressed powders, they contain wax (that's what they're pressed with), which can build up on the face making your makeup look heavy and thick.

CONCLUSIONS: I strongly suggest you try not powdering your face immediately after you've just put makeup on at the beginning of the day. Rather, use it after the day goes by for touching up makeup. As your own natural oil spreads over the face, powdering will help reduce that slippery-looking shine.

Brushes

The reason I recommend brushes when applying eyeshadows, blushers and contours is because I only recommend powders and never cream. Creams are messy, hard to control, absorb into the skin, lose color as you wear them, are finger painted on so they can look streaky and, because you are supposed to set creams with a loose powder, why bother with two steps when you can just apply the blush in one with a powder from the start? Even if your skin is very dry, creams will cause more problems than benefits.

Description: All cosmetics have an appropriate tool that is essential to the successful application of that particular product. One of the major tools is the brush. Not those little doll-size applicators or sponge-tip sticks that come with eyeshadows, but good, full-size, thick-haired, soft-bristle brushes to help assure good, even application of the contour, blush and eye makeup. This is as good a time as any for you to throw away those little brushes that come packed with the

c) **Proper Use of Brushes**

Eyeliner

DO
Use the flat side of the brush.

DO NOT
Use the tip. Do not splay the brush.

Eyeshadow

DO
Use the flat edge of the brush.

DO NOT
Splay the brush.

Blush, Powder or Contour

DO
Use the full head of the brush.

DO NOT
Splay the brush.

compacts which are too small to match the size of anyone's cheek or eye.

The rules for choosing the right brush are: **THE BRUSH SHOULD MATCH THE JOB AND SIZE OF THE AREA IT IS TO BE USED ON!** Brushes should not be so stiff they scratch the face and yet not so soft as to be floppy and difficult to control. A good brush can make all the difference between a quick, smooth makeup job and a sloppy, streaky, time-consuming makeup struggle.

Application: The tendency is to use brushes in a rubbing or wiping motion on the face. Many women beat at their faces with a wild brushing motion as they attempt to apply their blush and eyeshadows. There truly is an easier way. Here are two reliable techniques to follow: **DO NOT** rapidly wipe, beat or rub the brush against the face. Inadvertently, you may be wiping off what you just put on, not to mention wiping off the foundation underneath. **DO** brush in short, purposeful motions that glide over the skin.

Wherever there is a distinct line where the brush stroke was placed, or you feel an urge to use your hand to blend what you've just applied, you are most likely not using the brush properly, or your brush is too stiff for a soft application and blending. (You may also have applied your foundation poorly, which means you need to read over that section again.) You should not be blending anything with your fingers, only your brush or the flat, square, thin sponge you used to apply your foundation.

WARNING: Something else that is critical to using brushes effectively, even though it may seem insignificant at first, is the way you pick up the powder on your brush before you apply it. NEVER SMASH YOUR BRUSH INTO THE POWDER. Rather, place your brush into the powder gently, without moving the bristles. You don't want to see the brush hair bend or splay. (See diagram C) Always stroke through the powder evenly and be sure to knock the excess powder off the brush every time before you apply it to the face. Knocking the excess powder off prevents applying too much color to the first place your brush touches on the face.

Pros: Brushes are the only efficient and logical way to apply blush, eyeshadows and, on occasion, lipstick.

Cons: There are none, unless of course you're using rotten brushes.

CONCLUSIONS: A wise investment for any makeup case would be good brushes.

Contouring

Contouring the face is the art of creating or increasing shadows on your face so the face appears to have more structure. It involves using brown tones of blush or shadow along the sides of the nose, at the sides of the forehead and under the cheek-bone to add color, definition and drama to the face. This style of shading has gone through various phases of popularity, sometimes in . . . sometimes out. Of late it seems to be both, depending on how much makeup you wear; it's in if you wear a lot of makeup and out if you wear less.

For the most part, the emphasis of contouring to reshape the face has somewhat died down. The likely reason for its recent demise is that believable-looking contouring is a difficult technique to master. Applying contour takes skill and patience, which is more than most women have time to deal with every morning. Even if you do decide to take the time, the frequent result is that contouring can end up looking like a stripe of brown powder under the blush. My strong recommendation is to think twice before incorporating this step into your daily makeup routine.

When you do choose to try contouring it is always done as a separate step with a completely different color and brush from the blush application. Pinks, reds and oranges are used in blushing, only brown tones are used in contouring. The safest contour shade to use is one that looks like your skin color when it is tan. A *soft* golden shade of brown is generally the perfect color to use when trying to accomplish realistic shadows on the face. Shades of grey-brown can look dirty and shades of red-brown and mauve-brown can look like a bruise.

The traditional areas you can choose to contour are under the cheekbone, at the sides of the forehead, at the temple area and down the sides of the nose. Here are some rules of placement to help you find and apply the areas to be contoured. (Refer to diagram D)

NOTE: Avoid contouring or shading along any portion of the jawline. After you've gone through all the trouble to find a foundation that leaves no line of demarcation at the jaw, it does not make sense to brush on a brown stripe there and hope people believe it looks like natural shadows. It is

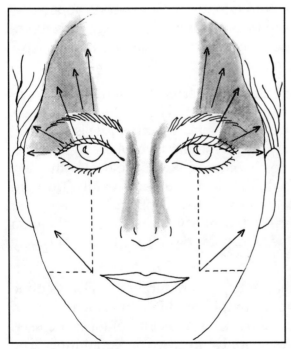

D) CONTOURING
Soften hard edges with your sponge. For temple contour reapply if needed to soften eyeshadow. Under cheekbone and nose, contouring is optional.

also wise to take into consideration the likelihood that makeup in this area will end up on your collar about 100% of the time.

Under The Cheekbone

To find this area you will need two thin pencils, diagram D and a well-lighted mirror. (You always need a well-lighted mirror when doing your makeup.) Take one of the pencils and place it vertically against the face in alignment with the pupil down along the cheek. Holding that in place take the other pencil and place it horizontally against the face parallel with your mouth from the corner of the lips to the ear lobe. Where these two pencils intersect is where your placement of the contour begins. This intersection should be approximately one-quarter inch behind your laugh line.

At this point place the center of your brush here and stroke the color straight back aiming towards the middle of the ear. You will find that these directions will put your color under the cheekbone. The area of application should be approximately one-half inch in width with no definite edges visible. Use your sponge to soften hard edges.

The starting point for under-cheekbone contouring is almost always the same because the cheekbone corresponds nicely to the eye socket and the jawline. The end point at the ear, though, can be varied depending on the effect you desire: The steeper the angle going towards the top of the ear, the longer the face will appear. A square- or round-shaped face might want to experiment contouring with a steeper angle. The longer the face, as an oblong- or triangular-shaped face might be, the more *straight* back towards the middle of the ear the line can be. This in effect deemphasizes the length of the face — not that deemphasizing is necessary, but neither is overemphasizing.

CAUTION: Be sure to never blend or place the contour color below the mouth, below the middle of the ear, or to raise it onto the cheekbone itself. There is also no need to try the technique of sucking in the sides of your mouth to help find your cheekbone, that will only help find the sides of the mouth, not the cheekbone.

RECOMMENDATION: The contour brush I recommend is the one usually labeled for blush or rouge. The traditional brush designated for blushing is too small for most cheeks so it becomes a poor choice for the purpose of applying blush. The brush labeled for contouring is also a poor choice because it is usually too hard and flat, which can make visible edges when applying your color. When contouring use the full of the rouge brush, knocking off the excess powder before applying and brushing in short quick motions; going back to the ear should net the best results.

Sides Of The Nose

The goal with this step is to make the contour color as soft as possible, while keeping it restricted to the sides of the nose at the same time. Be sure not to accidentally blend the color on the area under the eyes or on the face. Take extra care to blend only a small amount of contour color on such an obvious focal point of the face.

A good way to find where to place the brush is to take your index finger and lay it flat along the center of your nose. With your finger still in place take your brush and apply the contour along the side of it — where the brush falls against your finger is the area to be contoured. Once you've done this remove your finger and softly apply the contour fully around the tip of the nose and on the flare of the nostrils. Following the diagram continue the contour up under the eyebrow avoiding the tear-drop area and the center area between the eyebrows. This end point under the eyebrow will be an overlap spot for when you start applying your eyeshadows.

For the nose contour, either use a very large flat eyeshadow brush or use the brush you used for the under-cheekbone contour and pinch it thin enough to accommodate the sides of the nose.

Contouring the nose has nothing to do with whether the nose is large or small. There is a more artistic reason for using this shading technique. If you're applying a full, classic makeup and the nose is ignored, you will have color everywhere on your face except for a white blotch in the center of the face. Contouring the nose helps to achieve color balance for the rest of the face when you choose to wear a formal full makeup application.

Temple Contour

Temple contour is a very traditional step in makeup that is as essential as mascara and as basic as blush. In any fashion magazine you will notice that most of the models have this step applied. This technique creates an area of color for the eyeshadow to blend into. When temple contour is neatly applied, the eyeshadow at the back of the eye doesn't end abruptly as a harsh-colored edge on a flesh-colored space. Without temple contour the forehead becomes a great white wall against the color background of the cheeks and eyes.

The temple contour is placed at the back third of the under-eyebrow bone out and up onto the forehead like a pie wedge without the edges. The color is applied directly over the eyeshadow colors and then brushed all the way back to the hairline, about three inches wide at its fullest point. (See Diagram D)

CAUTION: The three things that can make temple shading go wrong is first forgetting that this step begins at the **BACK** third of the under-eyebrow brushing right on top of AND over your eyeshadow colors. The second is not brushing the contour directly over the eyebrow itself and the last is angling the brush straight back in a one-inch stripe instead of a soft three-inch pie wedge. Temple contour is a softly shaded area and it should never look like a stripe.

Blushing

Blushing is an important, obvious part of almost any makeup routine, so to see it painted on like highway dividers is very frustrating. I urge you to take your time with this step because when this is on wrong, regardless of what other steps you do right, no one will notice anything else.

The parameters for finding the areas to be blushed are almost the same as for contouring under the cheekbone. Using this method can be a fail-safe way to apply blush. Again, start with your two pencils and a well-lighted mirror. Place one of the pencils vertically against the face in alignment with the pupil along the center of the cheek. Use the other pencil and place it horizontally at the underside of the nose parallel with the mouth from the nose to the center of the ear. At the intersection of these two points — down from the pupil and across from the tip of the nose — is where you begin your blush. This area will be approximately one-quarter to one-half inch behind the laugh line. Place the full of your brush here and then brush **DOWNWARDS** moving back towards the center of your ear, applying the color gently as you go. (See Diagram E)

NOTE: Applying your blush by brushing down as opposed to back and forth will eliminate achieving a stripe effect instead of a blush effect. The blush area should be about two inches thick with no hard edges. Always have your handy-dandy little sponge nearby to soften edges.

BLUSH SAFETY CHECK: Never blush the lines around the eye as it makes them look more evident, as well as red and irritated. Also do not blush below the mouth or the laugh lines. Blush is only for the cheekbone. There is never a reason to blush your nose, forehead, hairline or chin. Red noses are something you have after a cold, not something you apply to your face. Please avoid stripes of blush down the center of the forehead and chin as well. It's like wearing a shoe on your hand — that just isn't where it was intended to go.

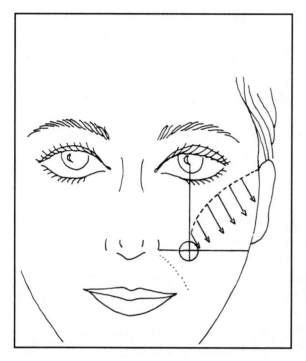

E) BLUSH PLACEMENT
Brush down and proceed back to ear. Do not blush by laugh lines or below mouth.

If you are applying both blush and under-cheekbone contour, you can apply the contour color first and then blend the blush on top of and gradually down into the contour color. Then, using your sponge, blend until you meld the colors together into an attractive design. The trademark of an attractive design is not being able to see where one color stops and the other color starts.

Eyeshadow Application

I developed an eyeshadow application sequence that can help you build the eye design of your choice in either one, two, three, four or five steps. The five steps are applied in colors that start light and become gradually darker corresponding with a specific area of the eye; the lighter color is placed all over the eye and then each subsequent darker shade is placed in smaller, more localized areas. To get through this sequence let's start with how to use eyeshadow brushes, how to choose where to place light and dark colors and then how to apply the design.

NOTE AND WARNING: Refer to diagram F for location of the terms used in the eyeshadow application descriptions. If any of the following descriptions are to make any sense at all, the diagrams must be referred to frequently for both information about placement and definition of terms.

USING BRUSHES: Eyeshadow, as far as application technique goes, is applied ONLY with brushes. Use small brushes that are designated specifically for eyeshadows. When you applied the contour and blush color you used the full of the brush; when applying eyeshadows you do just the opposite and use the flat side of the brush. Gently wipe the brush through the color, knock the excess out of the brush and apply to the eye with long, stroking motions. The movement is the action of laying strips of color that overlap each other, until an even, well-blended appearance is achieved over the entire eye area.

As always, **THE SIZE OF THE BRUSH MATCHES THE SIZE OF THE AREA YOU ARE WORKING ON;** if you have a large eyelid use a brush that is wide and full. If your eyelid is small the brush should be thinner in width and not so full. Brushes are an essential part of getting makeup on effectively and efficiently. Sponge-tip applicators or the small awkward brushes that come with cosmetics are the worst blending tools I've ever seen. Also avoid using brushes that have hard, coarse bristles or you will end up with hard lines and an irritated eyelid.

Designing The Eye

There are dozens of eye designs from which to choose that will create all kinds of effects. Be cautious of thinking you need to choose a design based on the need to *correct* a so-called problem of your eyes being too close together, too far apart, too round, not round enough or whatever. There are no standard facial dimensions that define how attractive you are. The best way to choose which design to wear is by how you want to be seen. Refer back to the Personality and Image Profile tests to help you determine how dramatic or subtle a makeup look you want.

Your own ability, personal preference and time consideration is the basis for choosing which eye design to start with. For example, if you're new to makeup, or prefer a near no-makeup look, use the one-color design with an eyeliner and temple contour. If you're used to wearing makeup, try starting with the four-color eye design.

The one- through five-color eye designs are step-by-step building blocks for completing a formal eye design — though each design by itself is a full design when worn with eyeliner, temple contour and mascara.

ONE-COLOR EYE DESIGN: One color is applied all over the eye area from the lashes to the under-eyebrow. This type of placement hopefully keeps you from wearing a splash of color only on the eyelid and ignoring the rest of the eye area. This design blends a soft, subtle color all over the eye leaving no patches of skin showing through.

Placing the shadow on the lid is fairly obvious. You place the color on evenly from the lashes to the crease being sure that you do not extend the color into the tear drop or out beyond the lashes. Also be certain there are no patches of skin showing through at the inside corner of the eye or next to the lashes.

The under-eyebrow area is a little more complicated. This area starts at the *instep* of the eye (see diagram F), where the eyebrow begins, next to the bridge of the nose. If you had applied a nose contour, that's where the contour color would have stopped and the under-eyebrow shadow placement starts. Regardless of whether you've contoured the nose or not, the underbrow color starts here; with the nose right there it provides a natural indentation that keeps the front edge of

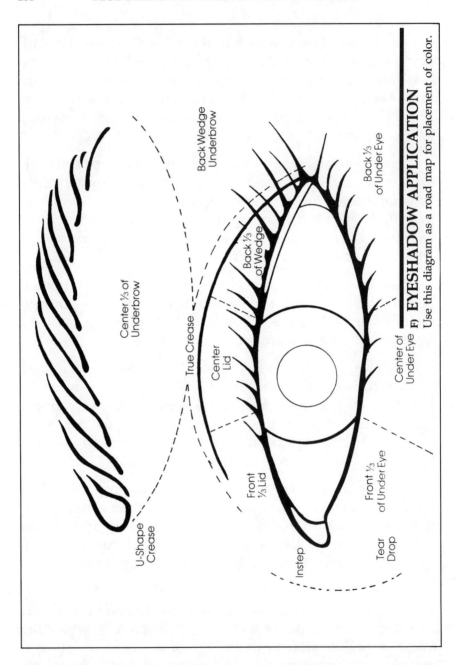

F) EYESHADOW APPLICATION

Use this diagram as a road map for placement of color.

your eyeshadow from looking too obvious. You apply the underbrow color from this inner corner by the nose, down to the crease, up into the eyebrow itself, blending out and across to the end of the brow and out into the temple contour. That's why the temple contour is also there, so that you won't see where the eye makeup starts and stops at the back of the eye.

Eyeliner and temple contour are required to complete the design. This single color should be a soft tan, neutral taupe, beige-brown, pale mauve-brown, etc., something definitely not obvious. Always avoid wearing a bright color all over the eye.

TWO-COLOR EYE DESIGN: In this design one color is applied fully on the eyelid and another separate color is applied fully from the crease to the brow. Follow the placement description for the one-color eye design. The lid color and under-eyebrow color in this design meet at the crease but do not overlap.

A liner and temple contour are required to complete the design.

WHICH COLOR GOES WHERE? When trying to choose which eyeshadow color goes where, there are two general rules to always keep in mind: **THE BIGGER THE EYELID, THE DARKER OR DEEPER THE COLOR CAN BE. THE SMALLER THE EYELID, THE BRIGHTER OR MORE VIVID THE COLOR CAN BE.** If the eyelid is already prominent it isn't necessary to make it appear any bigger. If the eyelid is small it is more than appropriate to put on a color that is more noticeable.

This same general rule applies for the under-eyebrow area. **THE SMALLER THE AREA UNDER THE EYEBROW, THE BRIGHTER THE COLOR SHOULD BE. THE LARGER THE AREA BETWEEN THE EYEBROW AND THE CREASE, THE DEEPER OR DARKER THE COLOR SHOULD BE.** If the area under the eyebrow is about the same as the lid the choice is yours. Either may look fine.

CAUTION: Never use shiny white, plain white or iridescent colors anywhere on the eye.

THREE-COLOR EYE DESIGN: Start with the one- or two-color eye design, following those directions closely. Once you have done that you would then add your third color choice in either a back wedge OR U-shaped crease design. What, you are asking, is a back wedge OR U-shaped crease design? They are the most classic ways I've found to shape and define the eyes. Because the next two designs also use the back wedge and U-shaped crease design I'll describe them after the five-color eye design.

For the three-color eye design, the lid and under-eyebrow color are softer and less intense than the wedge or U-shaped crease color.

To complete this design you would need to include a temple contour and eyeliner.

FOUR-COLOR EYE DESIGN: Start again with the one- or two-color eye design, then add a U-shaped crease color AND a back wedge. When both a U-shaped crease color and a back wedge color are used, the back wedge color is more intense or darker than the crease color.

To complete this design you would need to include a temple contour color and an eyeliner.

FIVE-COLOR EYE DESIGN: Start with a one- or two-color eye design, add a back wedge color and a U-shaped crease color, and last, a true crease color. (See diagram F) In order of least-intense color to most-intense color: The lid and under-eyebrow are light, the U-shaped crease color is slightly darker and the wedge and true crease color are the most intense.

Back Wedge

The back wedge is an accent color which shades either the back-third corner of the lid only and doesn't extend anywhere, or it can shade the back-third corner of the lid and extend out into the under-eyebrow and temple contour area. When only the back third of the lid is shaded it is called a back wedge. When the back-third corner of the lid is shaded, and then that same color extends softly into the crease, and out towards the back third of the under-eyebrow (where it overlaps with the contour color), it is then called a FULL BACK WEDGE.

The trick to getting the back wedge on correctly is to be sure you are in control of the color placement. Knock the excess off your brush and place the color on in very small strokes

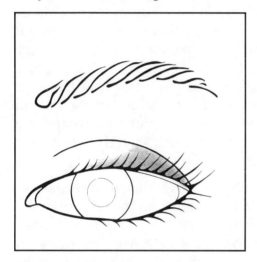

G) WEDGE
Shade the back ⅓ of the lid only.

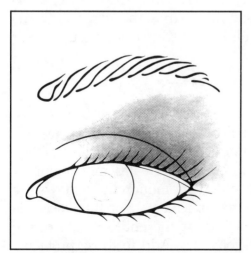

H) FULL BACK WEDGE
Shade from back ⅓ of lid out to the back ⅓ of the under-eyebrow. Temple contour blends out back edge of eyeshadow.

only over the back third of the lid. The problem with control is keeping the color on the back part of the lid area only. If you don't know how to handle the brush you can end up accidentally having the back wedge over more than half of the eye-lid or smudged out into the temple area, which, at least for this design, is not where you want it. (See diagram G)

The trick to applying the FULL back wedge is, once again, an issue of control and blending ability. Start first by applying your shadow to the back wedge area only on the back third of the lid. Once that is applied, without putting more powder on the brush, blend the back wedge shadow from the lid out towards the underbrow and temple contour area. It is essential that you not make this full back wedge look like a stripe or a smudge. (See diagram H) It is also important that the most intense placement of color is on the back third of the lid and not under the eyebrow. As you blend the full back wedge into place out on the under-eyebrow, this area should be the softest part of the color placement.

Another hint to doing the full back wedge correctly is to watch the angle of your brush as you blend the color from the lid towards the under-eyebrow area. If you place your color straight up in a 90° angle, you will look like you drew on wings. The softer the angle, the softer the appearance, so be certain you blend out and slightly up from the lid area towards the under-eyebrow. The full back wedge color should never reach the brow itself.

U-Shaped Crease

The U-shaped crease design is a wonderful look to achieve but very difficult to accomplish. The wonderful part of this design is that it shades, defines and creates movement by adding a shadow in a curved flowing motion that follows the natural shape of the eye. The difficult part of this design is blending this crease color on across the entire length of the eye without making it look obvious. Add to those problems

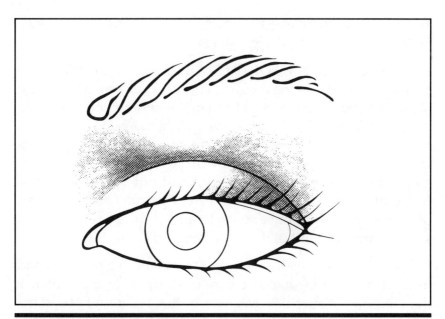

I) U-SHAPED CREASE
This design always includes a Full Back Wedge

---

the fact that the U-shaped crease color is darker than the lid and under-eyebrow color and you've got an interesting task to complete.

The U-shaped crease blends on from the front third of the under-eyebrow, sloping downward to the center true crease area and then gradually blending back up again to the back third of the under-eyebrow out into the temple contour. Of course this sweep of color needs to go on without looking like a stripe across the eye. The three places where you need to concentrate your effort are the area under the front third of the brow where the U-shaped crease color starts, the dip in the center to the crease and then deciding when to start your blending back up again toward the back third of the eyebrow. (See diagram I)

NOTE: I have vacillated between calling this design a U-shaped or an S-shaped design. When you look at the finished design it resembles a "U" but when applying, it goes on like an "S" due to the curved shape of the front third under-eye-brow area where the design starts.

SUGGESTIONS FOR RELIABLE APPLICATION: The center crease area is the darkest, so start your brush there and blend out and up to the front third of the under-eyebrow, being careful to keep this area soft and well-blended. When you've finished applying the color to the center crease and the front third of the under-eyebrow, place your brush back on the crease and then begin blending up and out to the back third of the under-eyebrow from this center point. The softest part of the design is the front and back third of the under-eyebrow, so be careful to not build up too much color in those areas.

The way to decide when to start blending the back and front part of the U-shaped crease color up from the center of the crease is to first discover where the eyebrow bone starts curving down. Look at one eye in a mirror. Now find your center crease. Notice that the center is the highest point and the rest of the crease curves down from there cresting around the shape of the eye. From this high center point, aiming away from where the crease begins curving downward, your blending movement should begin up towards the back third of the under-eyebrow or, in the other direction, up towards the front third of the under-eyebrow. This gives the illusion of lifting and opening the eye.

NOTE: Notice on diagram I that the U-shaped crease color always shades the back third of the lid just as you did in the back wedge design. This prevents the crease color from looking like a stripe hanging out in mid-air. The difference then between a three-color design, which gives you the option of using EITHER a U-shaped crease color or a back wedge color, and a four-color eye design, which utilizes BOTH the back wedge and the U-shaped crease color, is color selection. When the U-shaped crease is applied alone the back third of the lid is the same color as the crease. When both the back wedge and U-shaped crease are applied the back wedge is an entirely different or darker color than the shade used in the crease.

True Crease

A five-color eye design adds a true crease color to the full four-color eye design application. It is a deep color used in the fold of the eye that then connects with the back wedge on the lid. The true crease color is placed below the U-shaped crease color along the exact crease of the eye. The true crease color is always the most intense color of the eye design. The true crease and the back wedge color are often the same color.

The only trick to applying the true crease color is to not make it a pencil-thin stripe in the crease. It isn't a large area but it shouldn't be too thin either. Follow the crease exactly, stopping the brush before the tear drop, and follow all the way through in the crease at the back third of the lid.

CHOOSING WHICH COLORS GO WHERE: You already know that the lid color should be lighter than the under-eyebrow when the lid is smaller than the under-eyebrow. Or the lid should be somewhat darker than the under-eyebrow when the lid is larger than the under-eyebrow area. The back wedge and the U-shaped crease should be a darker or richer color than both the lid and under-eyebrow color. If you use both the back wedge and U-shaped crease design, the U-shaped crease color should be softer than the back wedge. The idea is to choose colors that are progressive shades of light to dark in the same color family, rather than choosing colors that are radically different from each other. Which is hard to do when most colors at the cosmetic counters come packaged in duo compacts that don't work together, like pink and green, or yellow and purple, or blue and pink.

Start with a soft beige color on the lid, then use a slightly darker tan-beige color under the eyebrow, followed by a taupe or grey-brown shade in the crease and a slate grey in the back wedge. If you want to try a more colorful array of shadows you can use a pale lavender on the lid, a soft mauve-brown under the eyebrow, a deep grey-lavender in the U-shaped crease and a rich purple on the back wedge. Always be careful when using vivid eyeshadow colors — they look more obvious than the more neutral brown, grey or tan shades of shadow. If you want to wear a more obvious color only one is necessary and the back wedge is a safe place to apply it.

REMEMBER: Watch your blending, you're actually never as concerned with where your makeup starts and stops as you are with how each application of shadow overlaps and blends into the other. What you want is smooth movement so that the eye travels over the face without stopping or tripping over lines, stripes, patches or streaks.

WARNING: To make this whole process as easy as possible, use colors that blend easily and always use the temple contour brush, not your sponge, to soften the back edge of your eye makeup. To assure yourself guaranteed success, avoid like the plague glittery, iridescent and shiny eyeshadows. Shiny eyeshadows exaggerate the lines on the eye, making you look wrinkly even when you don't have wrinkles.

Eyeliners

Let's take a short trip down eyeliner memory lane: Between 1960 and 1974 we progressed from wearing heavy liquid liner that swept over the eyelid ending in wings at the back of the eye, to wearing *Twiggy* lashes — which were pointy lines drawn vertically from the lower lashes with false eyelashes worn on the lid. Then, somewhere around 1976 the smudge pencils came into fashion. The smudge sticks were great; they were fast and convenient and, sad to say, did just what their name said they would do; they smudged all over the place. Smeared eye makeup was a definite problem.

Then there was the period between the late '70s and the early '80s when a fashionable eye was one where the liner was placed on the inside rim of the eye. We were told that placing the pencil here would make the white of the eye appear whiter.

Nothing could have been further from the truth. With constant application of a foreign substance in the eye, the resulting irritation leaves the eye bloodshot. Plus, this lovely effect of lining the inside rim only lasts about one hour and then the color clumps up at the inside corner of the eye and smears under the eye. Clumpy, smeary, bloodshot eyes are never fashionable, nor are they the least bit attractive. Thank goodness during the mid '80s eyeliner has become a more specific, though soft, line around the outside of the eyes.

WHAT KIND OF EYELINER TO USE? Because of all the problems I just mentioned with regard to pencils, I rarely recommend them for eyelining. Also, pencils are hard to sharpen, which makes it difficult to control the size of the line you want to apply. But not so with a brush and a powder. Whenever you're lining the eyes, I strongly recommend using a dark-toned eyeshadow color and a tiny brush. The tiny brush allows absolute control over the thickness of the line around the eye. Another benefit to using powder and a brush is that you can always use the powder as an eyeshadow or contour, depending on what color it is, by just changing the brush size.

HOW TO APPLY A POWDER EYELINER. Choose a dark shade of eyeshadow. Always line the eyes last after all the other eyeshadows are applied. Use a thin slightly stiff brush. Whether you use your powder WET or dry (preferably dry), stroke the brush through the color keeping the bristles together. Do not dab the brush or rub the brush into the color. Move it across the shadow in the direction of the bristles making sure the form of the brush is not destroyed (see diagram C). Knock the excess color from the brush and then apply to the eyelid next to the lashes or under the eye near the lower lashes.

When lining the eyelid make the line a solid, even line, starting thin at the front third of the lid, becoming slightly thicker at the back third of the lid. You can line all the way across the eyelid, from the inside corner to the outer edge, or you can choose to stop the line where the lashes stop and start. I prefer to line all the way across.

Along the lower lashes, line only the outer two-thirds with a softer color from the liner you used on the lid. Wrapping a complete eyeliner circle around the eye tends to create an eyeglass look and strongly changes the definition and softness. It can make the eyeliner the stronger statement rather than the eye itself.

HOW THICK CAN YOU LINE THE EYE? The thickness and intensity of the liner on the lid depends on the size of the lid — the larger the lid the thicker and softer the eyeliner should be. The smaller the lid the thinner and more intense the liner should be. When your lid doesn't show at all forget lining altogether.

WHICH EYELINER COLOR TO USE? The general rule for choosing a shade of eyeliner is to choose a brown, grey or black eye-shadow. Eyeliner is meant to give depth to the lashes and make them appear thicker. If the liner is a bright or true pastel color, the attention will be focused past the lashes to the colored line as opposed to the more subtle flow of color from dark lashes to dark liner. Test it on yourself. Line one eye with a vibrant color, the other eye with a brown or black and see which one looks like it has thicker lashes. Then, if all my attempts to convince you otherwise have failed and you still prefer to use bright pastel color liners, these basic application techniques are suitable for those colors as well.

Another important tip for getting eyeliner on correctly is to make sure the lower liner is less intense than the upper liner and that the two lines meet at the back corner of the eye. Do not extend the lines beyond the eye; please, do not draw on eyeliner wings by mistake or intention.

Drippies

Last, but not least, after the eye design and eyeliner are completed, check for drippies under the eye and on the cheek. Those are the little powder flakes that fly off the brush and land on the cheek. Knocking off the excess from the brush every time helps prevent drippies but there's always one or two flakes that end up where they don't belong.

Mascara

Mascara is a wonderful invention and is considered basic to all makeup applications. Many experts, including myself, say that if you're not wearing any other makeup but still want to wear something, wear mascara. On the other hand, many of us, and I'm guilty of this one too, get carried away and wear way too much mascara.

The need to overdo lashes is probably because most women feel long lashes are to be coveted and the cosmetic industry advertises this point to death. More mascara means longer, thicker, lashes right? Wrong! The more mascara you apply means the greater the chances are of the mascara flaking or chipping and for the lashes to appear hard and spiked. The eyelashes can only take so much weight and the excess weight can break them. Gunked up lashes with tons of mascara do not resemble long, thick lashes — they resemble gunked up mascara.

The desire for longer more noticeable lashes brings up the ever-popular device that curls the lashes by squeezing them into a bent-upward shape. The problem with curling lashes is that it can place the lashes at a severe angle which looks unusual, and for the sake of making lashes look longer, ends up breaking and pulling them out. Doesn't that defeat the purpose of making your lashes look longer?

Description: Mascara comes in three basic types: waterproof, water soluble and lash-lengthening. I prefer water soluble only.

Cons: Waterproof mascara causes problems because it doesn't dissolve in water. In order to remove this type mascara you must pull and wipe at the eye, which sags the skin and can pull out lashes. The other concern about waterproof mascara is that if it were indeed waterproof and some flaked into your eye the water in the eye wouldn't be able to dissolve the mascara and it could possibly scratch the cornea.

Lash-lengthening mascaras that contain fibers cause the same problems as waterproof mascaras, only worse. Even if the mascara itself is water-soluble the fibers usually aren't and they can severely scratch the eye. In fact, due to a lot of scratched corneas, it is hard to find mascaras that contain fibers anymore. Nowadays most lash-lengthening type mascaras are not all that different from any other mascara.

Pros: Water-soluble mascaras do not pose any of those hazards. They are easily removed by your water-soluble cleanser with no need to pull or rub the skin. When mascara falls into the eye, water-soluble types will dissolve with the water so there is little chance they can scratch the eye.

Application: Apply mascara to the lower lashes by holding the wand perpendicular to the eye and parallel to the lashes, which avoids getting mascara on the cheek. This makes it easier to reach the lashes at both ends of the eye. Both the traditional application of mascara, round-brushing the upper lashes from the base of the lash up, and holding the wand perpendicular at the edges can get all the lashes around the eye. Keep an old, cleaned up mascara wand in your makeup bag to be used for removing mascara clumps and separating lashes.

WARNING: Mascara mistakes landing on the skin can often be simply taken care of with most water-soluble mascara. Wait until the mistake dries completely and then chip the mascara away with a cotton swab or your sponge. Most of it will just flake off, with very little repair work needed. Always check for mascara smudges, they can look very sloppy and distracting.

Extending Longevity: The tendency for the mascara tube to dry up can be alleviated by not over-pumping the wand into the tube in an attempt to build up mascara on the brush. All that really accomplishes is pumping air into the tube, which makes the mascara dry up faster. Another solution is to avoid the wider-bristled mascara brushes. In order to accommodate the wider brush, the tube opening needs to be larger and this allows more air to get inside, causing the mascara to dry out faster. Don't be fooled by the hope that wider bristles will make lashes any longer, because that doesn't affect the application. If anything, when the brush applicator is too big it becomes clumsy to use and then it's harder to get the lashes at the corners without making mistakes.

You can increase the life of your mascara by adding a drop of distilled water to the tube. This can be repeated several times till all the mascara is gone. This, of course, applies only to water-soluble mascara.

NOTE: Mascaras are not supposed to smudge, flake or clump. It is not your fault if they do. Expensive mascaras do not tell you anything about a mascara's application. Drugstore mascaras can be as good as anyone else's, maybe better. Try a few until you find one you like.

Blue Eyelashes?

As I'm sure you've already guessed I'm not going to suggest you use blue, purple or green mascara. Aside from the fact that no one really has purple or blue lashes, this book is dealing more with classic makeup looks, and purple eyelashes would hardly constitute a traditional look.

Mascara is meant to enhance the eyes, not the lashes. Multicolored mascaras, like colored eyeliners, become a distraction and can make you look at the lashes separate from the eye. If you want the lashes to appear thick and shape the eye it is important that the mascara be a similar intensity and color to the eyeliner so that they flow from one to the other without a distinct separation. With that information, the only decision left is when to use black, dark brown or light brown. You determine that choice by the color intensity of the other makeup you're wearing. If you're applying black liner and dramatic eye makeup then use black mascara. A soft daytime makeup is perfect for brown liner and dark-brown mascara.

NOTE: If you have blonde hair, blonde lashes and blonde eyebrows, use light-brown mascara and a soft-brown liner. A blonde woman with very dark brows and dark lashes can use black or dark-brown mascara depending on the intensity of the rest of the makeup.

Eyebrows

No other aspect of makeup has gone through such dramatic fashion changes as eyebrow styles. We've gone from over-tweezed, pencil-thin, tortured brows to over-drawn, thickly penciled brows to, finally, a very soft, full, virtually tweezer free eyebrow. The idea is to think of eyebrows as being natural in appearance with no obvious tweezed line etched into the shape.

A full natural eyebrow is not only more attractive, it is also easier to keep up. Of course that doesn't mean you should have one thick line of eyebrow growing across the nose from one hair line to the other. We are talking natural not Neanderthal. There is a mid-ground between Groucho Marx and Greta Garbo when it comes to the shape of your brows.

Creating A Soft Eyebrow: Discovering the best shape for your eyebrow is very important. The shape and length of the eye itself is framed by the arch, length and thickness of the eyebrow. As much as a moustache can change the appearance of a man's face, so does the shape of an eyebrow affect the appearance of the eyes. For example, if you tweeze too much off the front part of the eyebrow the brows and eyes will appear smaller. Or if you tweeze too much away from under the eyebrow increasing the distance between the eye and the eyebrow you can look as if you are permanently raising your eyebrow in a surprised expression.

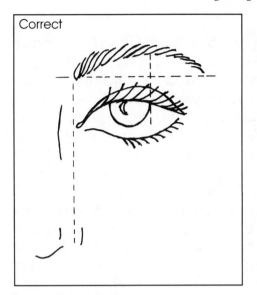

Correct

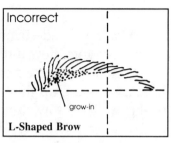

Incorrect
grow-in
L-Shaped Brow

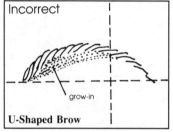

Incorrect
grow-in
U-Shaped Brow

J) EYEBROW

The eyebrow is correct when the arch falls over the back ⅓ of the eye and the front ⅓ of the brow starts from the center of the nostril.

L-Shaped Brow
Problem: Arch is over front ⅓ of brow.
    Cure: Grow-in or powder indicated area.

U-Shaped Brow
Problem: No arch.
    Cure: Grow-in or powder indicated area.

Over-Extended Brow (back)
Problem: Back ⅓ of brow is lower than front ⅓ of brow.
    Cure: Grow-in or powder indicated area. Tweeze indicated area.

Over-Extended Brow (front)
Problem: Front ⅓ of brow is lower than back ⅓ of brow.
    Cure: Tweeze indicated area.

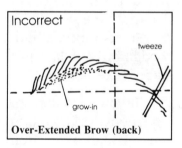

Incorrect
tweeze
grow-in
Over-Extended Brow (back)

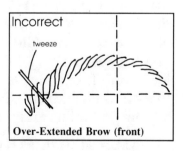

Incorrect
tweeze
Over-Extended Brow (front)

Making the decision of which hairs to leave and which ones to remove is the difference between an attractively shaped brow and a misshaped one. You can use a pencil and diagram to help you line up the following parameters for shaping your eyebrow. The brow should begin in alignment with the center of the nostril. The arch should fall at the back third of the eye and, although the eyebrow should be as long as possible, it still shouldn't end into the temple area. The basic rule to follow is: **THE FRONT PART OF THE BROW SHOULD NEVER DROP BELOW THE BACK PART OF THE BROW AND VICE VERSA!** Allowing this to happen, either with the way you tweeze your eyebrow or draw it on, makes you look like you're frowning or overemphasizes the downward movement of the back part of the eye.

Shading Your Eyebrow: To apply eyebrow color, use a soft-textured powder and a soft wedge brush following the same guidelines as above for tweezing. I never recommend using eyebrow pencils. They can produce a greasy look, tend to mat the hair, and usually look like a leftover from the 1930s. To apply the powdered brow color, brush the brow up with an old toothbrush and then apply the color with an angled wedge brush filling in the shape of the brow in between the hair where needed.

If you need to reshape your eyebrow a good rule to follow on where to place the color along the brow is: If your eyebrows are set high away from the eye, place the color under the eyebrow. The closer the brow is to the eye, the more you keep the color towards the top of the brow. Only work with the hair that is there. **SHADE, RATHER THAN DRAW, NO FURTHER AWAY THAN 1/4 INCH FROM WHERE THE NATURAL HAIR GROWTH STOPS.** No one believes the line extended beyond the natural shape is a real brow. It simply looks very fake and accentuates the fact that there is no brow there in the first place. Eyebrow is a suggestion, a shadow of a brow, not a line and not an obvious application of color.

MATCH THE COLOR YOU APPLY TO THE BROW

COLOR ITSELF RATHER THAN TO YOUR HAIR COLOR.
You don't want to see a separation between the eyebrow hair and the shadow used to fill it in. If you have pale eyebrows and want to darken the brow color use a soft shade of brown that is close to your brows' natural color. If you have red hair and brown eyebrows, using a red pencil or red-brown powder will look unnatural. A woman with blonde eyebrows may use a slightly darker blonde or taupe color on her brows to make them visible. The goal is to use what we have as the basis for makeup application, not to make an obvious theatrical change.

If you don't have much of an eyebrow present use the wedge brush and powder following the bone above the eye, using whatever little hair is there. Usually there's enough shape to create a natural, shaded impression of a brow. Use a light touch, short quick motions, and avoid the temptation to exaggerate the shape, arch it severely, or extend it into the temple. Downplay the fact that there is no hair and don't overexaggerate it with a strong, eye-catching line. Also, don't place a highlighter or light-colored eyeshadow under the brow to delineate further the placement of the brow color. Something dark next to something light makes it look more prominent.

Shaping The Brows With Mascara: An option for sparse, light-colored eyebrows is to brush mascara that matches the color of the brow through the brow to make it appear thicker. It will take a few times to get the hang of it. You might have trouble at first controlling the amount of mascara from the tube to the brow. Try using an old, slightly dried-up mascara instead of a new one; it will make it easier to apply the right amount. Give it a try, it can really work.

Lipstick And Lipliner

Most of you already know this one, but I've also talked to enough women to know that this next comment needs mentioning: Simply put, if you're wearing makeup your lips will need lipstick, not lip gloss, lipstick. Lip gloss is for teenagers who are not supposed to be wearing makeup. Lipstick is for adults who want to look polished and put together. Naked lips with madeup eyes or cheeks can look like you forgot you had a mouth. For the sake of balance, remember your mouth.

When you wear lipstick, a lipbrush or lip pencil are optional mouth accessories. Lipliner helps to draw on a definitive edge around the mouth to follow when applying lipstick, and a lipbrush helps control your application. The lipstick tube itself is too big for some lips and too small for others. If your lips are small it is best to use a lipbrush; if your lips are large the only reason to use a lipbrush is for improved accuracy.

When using a pencil lipliner always place the color on the actual outline of your mouth. Do not use corrective techniques that make the mouth look larger or longer, especially for daytime makeup. If you try to change the outline of your mouth with a lip pencil by drawing it on the outside of the lips, two hours later when your lipstick wears off, the lipliner, which tends to last longer than the lipstick, will still be in place and it will look like you missed your lips. Always line the lips following the actual shape, then fill in with your lipstick color using either the tube or lipbrush.

FASHION NOTE: Lipliner stopped being an obvious, dark, brown or definite line around the mouth over a decade ago. (Brown lipliners and lipsticks weren't attractive colors when they *were* in fashion.) Using a lipliner should not be an obvious line that shows up as a colored border around the lipstick. The goal is to have the lipstick and lipliner meld so that you cannot see where one starts and the other stops. The benefit of the lipliner is to place a more permanent color on the lips than the lipstick that won't wear off as fast as the lip color does.

When choosing the color of lipstick to wear follow these basic rules: Thinner lips need to wear brighter more vivid colors and avoid darker shades. Deeper colors on thin lips make the mouth look severe and harsh. Larger lips can wear just about any color, but the softer brighter shades are more fashionable and usually more versatile than darker colors.

Brighter colors may take a bit of getting used to, but once you do they truly make the mouth look softer and more attractive.

Stop Your Lipstick From Traveling Into The Lines Around Your Mouth: To stop lipstick from bleeding the first thing to do is avoid greasy lipsticks and lip glosses. The greasier the lipstick and lipliner are, the faster the color will slip into the lines around the mouth. Drier-feeling lipsticks are best for conquering this problem. Powdering the mouth with loose powder before applying the lipstick also helps. Another trick is to line the mouth slightly smaller than it actually is. This technique takes into account that lipstick moves as you wear it, so why start out placing the color where it will eventually end up anyway? Initially placing the liner inside the edge of the mouth will keep the lipstick from getting past this area sooner than it would if you started at the edge in the first place.

A few years ago some cosmetic companies came out with a new product that was supposed to prevent lipstick from bleeding. These never worked for me. I found them thick and uncomfortable — like I had something on my lips I couldn't get off, and my lipstick still found its way into the lines around my mouth. The present lack of availability of these products indicates that they didn't work for a lot of people besides just me.

RUMOR BUSTING: There is no truth to the story you may have heard that using a lipstick brush helps keep the lipstick on longer. Why the brush would serve this purpose has never been explained to me in a manner that makes any logical sense. Lipstick stays on longer when you put on "a lot" of lipstick, wear strong vivid colors that are not greasy, and avoid wearing lip glosses. Those things will definitely keep lipstick on longer.

Is There A Difference Between Lipsticks? Yes, there are vast differences between lipsticks. But there are no differences between lipsticks from one cosmetic line to another. As you probably already know from experience lipstick colors and textures can vary within the same cosmetic line. Some are creamy, others are dry, greasy, shiny, flat, melt easily, go on sticky, smeary, evenly, thick, thin and combinations thereof. The lipsticks I recommend should go on creamy in an even layer that doesn't smear or look thick. The only way to discover this for yourself is to be patient and try on the colors you like and see how they feel.

How Much Makeup?

It is completely up to you how much makeup you choose to wear. But to make that decision a useful one and not a passing whim, base how much makeup you wear on the image you want to project. Makeup, like clothing, impacts the observer with a statement of intention. Wearing a business suit instead of a jogging outfit to an office meeting makes a definite statement and it would make an even bigger statement if you were to do it the other way around. Because people react to the way we look and because makeup is a part of how we look, makeup, whether we like it or not, reveals something about who we are. To be sure the way you look is saying what you want it to, the concept of balance is essential to keep in mind when deciding what is right for you.

Balance is the way several different things work together to create one statement. Using the clothing analogy of wearing a business suit or jogging suit to the wrong occasion can apply to makeup the same way, because a fully applied makeup with a jogging outfit is as inappropriate as no makeup with a business suit.

Matching Your Makeup To Your Personality

When my friend Sheri, who helped me review this section and is also the consummate Enthusiast, finished her last comments, she exclaimed, "I could never do all of this, it is so complicated and involved, I can't even find my face in the morning much less the different sections of my eye that you describe!" I turned to her and said, "Spoken as a true Enthusiast. Anything that takes time to master is too much trouble. It has to be fast and most of all fun. If there were a makeup party going on you would be there in a minute and hang around for hours telling stories, but heaven forbid you should spend the time seriously learning how to do something in a truly effective manner!" After we wiped the tears of laughter from our eyes she acknowledged that detail and things that seemed boring to her were always too much trouble to bother with. We then turned the conversation around to how she could overcome her resistance to learning the details of a good makeup application.

Enthusiasts need to realize that details become second nature as ability and comprehension take the place of boredom. Also, in the long run, the entire makeup routine should only take 5 to 15 minutes depending on which steps you choose to do. The way for Enthusiasts to overcome their considerations of time is to remember that completing something can be exciting in and of itself. Patience is not always a boring attribute, it sometimes achieves desired results.

In contrast the Controllers love fashion detail and the chance to master a more interesting, sophisticated look. However, if the Controllers are too busy or too convinced that what they are presently doing is the *right* routine for them, they won't bother to try something new. Opening up to change that isn't readily apparent seems like a waste of time to Controllers. The simple way for Controllers to incorporate the makeup ideas I've presented is, when they get the time, take a close look at their makeup routine and evaluate if the results are really what they want. If the liner is looking smeared and the blush choppy it might be time to take the time to change.

Analyzers are the most easy to please with choices and techniques. They will simply pick and choose the ones they feel fit, patiently figure out how to do them and wear them the same way confidently every day.

Supporters don't have to be convinced one way or the other because they never bought this book in the first place or they stopped after they finished the skin-care section. Supporters understand the importance of clean skin but they find the formality of makeup hard to deal with. For those Supporters who did finish this makeup section consider starting bit by bit with one step at a time. There is no reason to do everything if you don't want to.

Here are some suggestions to help each personality group find a comfortable place to begin: Supporters — can wear a soft shade of lipstick, brown mascara and a soft shade of eyeliner around the eye. Enthusiasts — can wear a mini-application of foundation, blush, temple contour, the three-color eye design with a colorful back wedge, an eyeliner, mascara and vivid shade of lipstick. Controllers — can do it all being careful not to overdo. Analyzers — can wear a mini-application of foundation, a soft blush, a one-color eye design, eyeliner, mascara and a bright shade of lipstick.

REMEMBER: When choosing which makeup items or colors you want to use, the art of makeup is the flow of color and line on the face from one area to another so the viewer's eye never rests on any particular aspect of the application. Lining the eyes with black liner and not balancing it out with vivid lipstick and blush will not look finished. The same is true for lots of blush color with one eyeshadow color or a pale lipstick.

— Chapter Eight —
The Last Hurdle

Choosing Colors That Work

Makeup Theory 2 — **FASHION MAKEUP MEANS CHOOSING COLORS THAT GO TO-GETHER.** It is obvious from the sheer number of makeup colors available that there is no one universally accepted opinion as to the *best* way to combine color. There are so many differing options and preferences that it's not only unlikely you will ever find the *perfect* combination, but unnecessary. Just as there isn't one color combination of clothing you wear every day, the same is true for your makeup. Yet there are ways to go about making two or three good choices that should solve most of your makeup wardrobe needs. Here are some of the most efficient and aesthetically reliable rules.

Rule Number One: Color-dress your face the same way you would color-dress your body. If you wouldn't consider wearing a pink skirt with a blue blouse and an orange jacket, don't wear those colors on your face. This means you should avoid wearing orange lipstick, blue eyeshadow and pink blush. It even sounds distracting. As much as possible work *monochromatically* when using colors for the lips, cheeks and eyes. Dress your face so it doesn't clash with itself. If your blush and eyeshadows are mauve, lavender and grey (blue undertone), so should the lip color be in the same blue undertone color family. The lipstick then can be either pink or mauve or some other soft shade of a blue undertone color. If your blush and eyeshadow are rust and peach in color (yellow undertone), so should the lipstick be either peach, rust, pale orange or red with yellow undertones.

Rule Number Two: Dress your face so it doesn't clash with what you wear. Matching makeup to your clothing is important. The same way you wouldn't wear a pair of orange shoes with your pink skirt, do not wear an orange shade of lipstick with your pink outfit. That doesn't mean if you're wearing a blue skirt you should wear blue eyeshadow any more than it means for you to wear a blue lipstick. This very outdated notion about blue outfit equals blue eyeshadow falls apart when you wear a black, navy or red-and-white-striped outfit. What color blush, lipstick and eyeshadows are you supposed to wear then? The clothes you are wearing will always have a particular color undertone and your makeup colors should coordinate with that tone and nothing else.

The undertone of a color refers to how blue or yellow it is. All colors can have either blue or yellow undertones. For example: When grey has yellow undertones it can appear drab or ashen-green. When grey has blue undertones it can appear charcoal or slate grey. When brown has blue undertones it may appear rosy-brown, mauve-brown or charcoal-brown. When brown has yellow undertones it can appear neutral-beige to golden-tan or copper. When red has blue undertones it can appear pink, scarlet or fuchsia. When red has yellow undertones it may appear orange, coral or peach.

If your wardrobe is mostly neutral, without being overwhelmingly blue or yellow undertoned, you have a lot less to worry about when choosing makeup colors to coordinate with your clothing. Your makeup will blatantly clash with your clothing if it is an obvious color mismatch like a pink blouse and an orange lipstick or a peach blouse and a rose blush. Even though greys, blacks, tans and neutral colors of clothing do indeed have blue and yellow undertones, because they tend to be less obvious, they rarely clash with most colors of makeup. It is important to think of makeup as a fashion accessory and follow this rule of matching the undertone of your makeup with the undertone of the clothes you're wearing.

Rule Number Three: Do not wear makeup (or clothing) colors that are more intense or less intense than you are. For those of you who haven't been *seasoned* yet (discovered what clothing colors are best suited to your skin and hair color) or even if you have been, consider this simple, basic color compatibility idea: If you are blonde with fair skin, intense colors like black, cobalt blue, fuchsia or neon red will overwhelm you. Rather softer colors like grey, azure blue or pink would look more balanced. If you have dark hair and dark skin, pale blue or pink will make you look pale and blah. The stronger, more intense colors look best on women with dark hair and sallow or black skin.

If you are blonde and have dark skin or have dark brown hair with fair skin, stronger blue-undertoned colors would be great but you still would NOT want to go TOO intense. Auburn-haired women with fair skin almost always look better in vibrant rich colors that are yellow-based. Red-haired women with fair skin will want to look for colors that are soft, subtle and yellow-based. Grey-haired women with sallow skin can wear the bright vivid blue-toned colors and grey-haired women with fair skin can wear softer pastel blue-toned colors. Yellow tones are not the best for women with grey hair unless it is a vivid peach-pink color.

The Agony And The Ecstasy — Choosing Color

Choosing color can have its agonies even when you know all the color intensity rules. You need to be cautious not only of how you coordinate your makeup with your clothing, but you also need to be aware of how different makeup colors look in combination on your skin. Skin tone has a direct effect on the makeup colors you wear and the opposite of that is also true: Makeup colors have a direct effect on your skin tone. If you are looking for a pink (blue undertone) blush to wear it is important to realize how that color will make your skin look.

For skin that has strong yellow, brown or ashen-green tones, always avoid reinforcing those skin colors by using those colors on the face. Eyeshadows, lipsticks or blushes in shades of orange, peach, yellow, chocolate-brown, grey-green, rust, khaki or the like will only make sallow skin appear more sallow and pale. If your skin is ruddy and red in appearance, wearing colors of pink, purple, blue, red, rose, mauve and the like will only make the face look more red and more irritated.

SUMMARY: Sallow skin is better off wearing blue-under-toned colors only. Ruddy skin is better off wearing yellow-un-dertoned colors most of the time.

What If My Clothes Are The Wrong Color?

Even if the outfit you want to wear is a color that is not the most flattering for you, it is still necessary to find makeup colors that will not clash. For example, if you wear a vibrant purple outfit and the better color for you is a softer shade of lavender, choose eyeshadows in varying shades of lavender and grey with a pink blush that isn't vibrant pink and do the same with your lipstick. Those makeup colors will work with your outfit and be soft enough to go with your skin tone.

The same would be true for a woman who is wearing earthy, yellow-undertoned colors but should be wearing more vibrant blue-undertoned colors like hot pink or royal blue. In this situation choose colors of blush and lipstick that are a more vivid shade of coral-pink with eyeshadows that are a soft tan on the lid and under-eyebrow with a charcoal-grey crease and eyeliner color. Those colors should work with both the outfit and skin tone without clashing.

Is Fashion Awareness For Everyone?

At this point, mostly the Supporters and Enthusiasts are usual-ly ready to throw in the towel. Their comments are, "I don't want things that are fashionable, I just want to look good." Sorry, it's hard to have one without the other. For example, you might have looked really good in go-go boots and Nehru jackets 20-odd years ago, but today chances are they will look out of place. What is fashionable today is directly related to what looks good. Yet, within any fashion statement there are lots of clothing options to choose from that will look great on you and the same follows for makeup. Remember false eye-lashes, thick plastic eyeliner, white under-brow highlighter, dark-brown striped in the crease or dark-brown lipstick? Those are all out of style too. Yet there are dozens of other options that have taken their place which look wonderful today. The goal for you is to find what is comfortable, looks good and is fashionable all at the same time.

Blue Eyeshadow Should Still Be Illegal!

This is the perfect time to mention why I feel that blue eyeshadow should be illegal. Blue is probably the most misused makeup color women wear, although shiny lime-green and bright shiny pink eyeshadows run a close second, with rosy, orange foundations close behind. But blue wins hands down because it is sold more than any other color in the country. (Do you get the feeling I might be fighting a losing battle?)

Solid blue splashed across the lid, or worse, painted all over the eye from the lashes to the brow, flashes out from the eye area like a neon sign. Blue is a difficult color to blend with any other color so it always tends to stand out and be more obvious than anything else you may have on. You can see a blue stripe across the lid from across the room! Not the eyes, not the face, just the blue eyeshadow.

In all fairness, I'm referring to a complete solid covering of bright blue eyeshadow over the eyelid or a bright blue eyeliner, thickly wrapped around the lashes. For some eye designs, a little shading at the back of the eye, or an eyeliner of navy or slate-grey blue, if done properly and with restraint, isn't the worst thing I can think of. (See, I really can be very flexible.)

If you feel you get compliments on your blue eyeshadow or liner then you definitely should reconsider how you wear your eye makeup. You want people to compliment you, not your eyeshadows. You may also want to take the time to flip through a fashion magazine and notice that none of the fashion layouts (the ads for the fashion designers, not the makeup ads) have models wearing blue eyeshadow, so why are you?

A Quick Review

Highlighter: Apply the white highlighter along the inside corner of eye with your finger or a cotton swab. If you are using a more fleshtone highlighter apply it after the foundation has been blended into place.

Foundation: Apply the foundation in dots over the central area of the face with either your fingertips or a sponge. Blend the foundation in place with the sponge. Use the edge of the sponge that doesn't have foundation on it to buff and remove the excess. Foundation blends over the white under the eye and on the eyelid. Avoid placing foundation on or near the jawline.

Brush Usage: Knock the excess powder off the brush before applying color to the face and use short quick blending motions. Never wipe or rub the brush across the face.

Contouring: Do before you apply the blush. Use a medium-sized blush brush. Be sure to never place the contour color near the jaw or on the cheekbone.

Blushing: Avoid placing the blush near the eye area. Use a large powder brush and apply the color in downward strokes moving back toward the ear.

Eyeshadows: The lid color is usually the lightest shade of color and goes on first, next is the underbrow color, which can be slightly darker than the lid color. After those two colors are applied you can apply either or both the U-shaped crease or back wedge color. These two shadows are the darkest part of the eye design.

Eyeliner: The eyeliner can be the same color as the back wedge or U-shaped crease color. The eyeliner goes on after the entire eye design has been applied. The lower liner blends on softer than the lid liner.

Mascara: Use brown, dark-brown or black mascara but do not overdo.

Eyebrows: Generally it is best to leave the eyebrow alone but if it is too thin or has been over-tweezed fill in the brow after the rest of the makeup is in place.

Lipstick: Line lips first and then apply the lipstick.

Blending: Check your blending with the sponge. No hard lines or drippies should be visible whatsoever.

Potential Problems

Highlighter problems are caused when you use too little or too much of it under the eye. Too little doesn't give enough coverage, and too much makes white rings around the eyes or slips into the lines, looking thick and smeary.

Foundation can be a problem if you apply too much or too little. Too little and the rest of the makeup will go on choppy; too much and it will look like a mask. Be careful to blend evenly and do not forget to cover the eyelid, especially the outer third (back corner) next to the eyelashes, the corners of the nose and around the mouth.

Foundation filling the lines on the face is primarily caused from using too much foundation or too heavy a foundation and then not blending it on thin enough. Use a lightweight water-based foundation always and blend well, using a clean edge of your sponge to go over the lines to pick up any excess foundation. Once the foundation is blended you can apply a light amount of loose powder over the lines to prevent the makeup from slipping into them. Be careful not to use too much powder or your makeup will look caked and thick.

If the face is much lighter or darker than the neck, you will need to follow the color of the neck when choosing your foundation color.

Red-brown (blue tones) contour colors should not be used for contouring. Red shading can make the skin look burnt and unnatural. Use only tan, taupe or yellow-brown tones when contouring.

If you have pale skin be sure to blend your blush and contour colors well to avoid stripes. You can also increase the area of the temple contour and blush to give the face a bit more color, just be subtle about it, don't overdo. If you have fair skin use softer colors of shadows, blush and lipstick. Darker shades of skin should be using stronger makeup tones. DURING THE SUMMER, IF YOU TAN, YOUR COLORS OF MAKEUP WILL NEED TO BE DIFFERENT FROM THE ONES YOU WORE DURING THE WINTER.

When blush goes on choppy it's usually due to one of three things: not enough foundation, poor blending technique with the brush from either over-blending (which wipes off the foundation), not knocking the excess off the brush (which puts too much color on the face) or using a blush shade that is too strong or too grainy (which tends to go on heavy and uneven).

If you are wearing the U-shaped crease color be careful not to use too dark or grainy an eyeshadow color or it will be difficult to blend on softly.

Pink eyeshadows on the lid will make you look like you've been crying. Shiny eyeshadows will make the eye look more wrinkled than it is. And don't forget to check for drippies after the eye design is complete.

What To Do If You Wear Glasses

Glasses can pose problems only if you don't realize how they can affect makeup. Depending on the type of prescription you wear, the lens will change the appearance of the eye. When the lens magnifies the eye, making the eye look larger, you will need to adapt your makeup so it doesn't appear harsh or overdone. Choose eye colors that are soft, being sure to avoid highly contrasting colors. Also apply the eyeliner softer in a smudged, less-defined line and avoid applying a heavy, thick coating of mascara.

If the lens demagnifies the eye you can increase the color and definition around the eye. But be careful, more color does not mean using blues or greens or leaving hard edges. Shades of blue and green or hard edges with this type of prescription glass will only look like a small hard edge and a small flash of color.

The frame of your glasses will also affect how you apply makeup. Be sure your blush is placed below the edge of the frame. You don't want the frame to break up the movement or angle of the blush.

─────── Chapter Nine ───────
Miscellaneous Touches

How To Shop For Makeup

Shopping for makeup can be very tricky. I am totally sympathetic to this dilemma because I know how messy, time consuming and frustrating this can be. There is truly only one way to prevent buying the wrong color: **TRY IT BEFORE YOU BUY IT** and do not buy anything because you were intimidated by the salesperson or because you impulsively decide you need it.

Trying makeup on to test the color only works if you put it on your face without other makeup color. It does no good to put makeup on over your other makeup; all that tells you is how a blush will look when worn over your present blush. Also, do not try makeup on over any other part of your anatomy besides your face. Your arm, wrist or ear is not your face.

Consider it this way: You wouldn't shop for a new piece of clothing by putting it on over the clothing you were already wearing, would you? And you wouldn't try a blouse on over your left leg to see if it fits! The same is true for your face. You must experiment with different makeup types and colors on a clean face or a face with only your foundation on to really see the effect of the cosmetics you want to buy.

Judging The Texture Of A Powder

One way to judge how a color will go on the skin is by feeling the texture of the powder itself. The drier or softer the feel of the powder, the less intense the application is likely to be. The heavier, greasier, or grainier the feel of the powder the more thick and intense the application will be. With softer-textured shadows and blush, more color will need to be added to build definition. With heavier-feeling powders, less color is needed to build definition.

NOTE: The greasy, heavy and grainy-textured powders can be very difficult to blend. Generally speaking it is best to use these as eyeliners or back wedge colors and nothing else. As a general rule: The heavier a color goes on or feels the better it will be for eyelining; the softer the color goes on, the better it will be for shading, contouring and blushing.

SECOND NOTE: Try mixing different textures of blushes and eyeshadows with each other or with a translucent powder to create new color options. You'll double the colors you have to work with by making them softer or darker.

What's In A Name?

When you buy a cosmetic you can be confident that a lipstick will be a lipstick and a foundation will be a foundation. However, when you try to buy a color of blush or foundation according to name alone, reality exits and fantasy enters.

The color name of a product reflects image, not color. When you spend $10.00 on a blush or a contour, brown doesn't sound as expensive or as exciting as *St. Tropez Tan* or *Terracotta*. Foundations may be called *Porcelain*, but what color is porcelain? My porcelain sink at home is white (well, usually white). A lipstick called *Cherries Jubilee* or *Bordeaux* is not helping you understand what color shade that is supposed to represent. Choosing color by name is truly frustrating and relatively useless. Choose color according to appearance, and how it looks once it's on the face is the only way to make a final decision.

Put My Blush Where?

Some women are still skeptical about using an eyeshadow on areas of the face for which the label says it was not intended. The concern is that the eyeshadow shouldn't be used as an eyeliner or a blush or that powder liner will stay on. Retailers would love for you to think that there is a vast difference between blushers and eyeshadows and that you can't use a product except for where the label tells you to. Most powders, whether they're called blush or eyeshadow, contain the same ingredients. Anything that would be harmful to your eyes would be specifically indicated on the package. Worry about color choice, not product type or name.

Makeup Bags — A Holding Tank

Most cloth makeup bags that are used to hold cosmetics are usually inefficient. Not only is it impossible to find anything in them, they can't hold everything. Especially when you consider the size of the typical compacts you buy. My suggestion: Purchase a makeup bag that is vinyl, so you can easily see what's inside, and has enough room to hold all your makeup. Buy a separate makeup bag that is also vinyl to carry a few touch-up items with you in your purse or briefcase.

Where Do You Put On Your Makeup?

Bathrooms can be the worst place to put on your makeup. If they're not steamy and damp then they are poorly lit. Either invest in good lighting or change locations to the best lighting source in the house. If the kitchen table has the best available light and you're concerned about making a mess or leaving your cosmetics lying around, buy a tray large enough that can transport and store all your makeup.

Cosmetic Acne

I've heard this term bandied about and I'm not sure the condition exists. Whether or not I use makeup I breakout, no more and no less. I've read and been told that I should have waited till my acne cleared up before I started wearing makeup, which would have meant I'd have never gotten started. If you are one of those women whose acne is a direct result of wearing makeup, usually the foundation or moisturizer is the culprit and you should stop wearing it immediately. But from my experience with thousands of women, when that is the case it is quickly remedied by finding another product that doesn't make you breakout.

In my opinion there are two major reasons something like cosmetic acne occurs, separate from an allergic reaction. The first is falling asleep while still wearing your makeup. That is one of the quickest ways to have problems even if your skin is the type that typically never has a blemish anywhere. The second is when a woman automatically assumes that because she is over a certain age she should be wearing a moisturizer. That misinformation can lead a direct path to clogged pores and some degree of acne. Dry skin needs moisturizer, everyone else can save their money.

NOTE: If you want to wear a sunscreen, you will have to experiment till you find one that doesn't make you breakout.

Choosing A Makeup Artist

I highly recommend taking the time to get your makeup done by a professional makeup artist and not just once but several times. Being born female doesn't mean you instinctively know how to put on blush and eyeshadow. It also isn't information handed down from generation to generation. If anything, our mothers had less information than we do.

Although getting your makeup done professionally is very important and incredibly helpful, the quality of the work you receive can vary greatly. Be prepared to work with the makeup artist as you would your hairdresser. Remember the haircuts you received when you sat down and told the hairdresser to do whatever he/she felt like?

In order to help you select a trained and thoroughly qual- ified makeup artist the following is a good checklist:

1. Referrals: How did Dolores turn out when she went? Check with people you know who have seen the makeup artist you're considering, that way you can have a sense of how they work. If possible, don't rely on newspaper ads or the Yellow Pages.

2. How does the makeup artist wear her makeup: if the artist is a woman, that is. Is it something you'd wish to emulate, or something you pray she doesn't do to you? That isn't necessarily a definitive sign, but remember we're looking for a process to narrow down the choices with. If the makeup artist is a man, ask to see examples of his work.

3. When starting, does the artist ask you about your lifestyle? Do you work in an office? Stay home with the children? Have any known allergies to makeup? A really good question to be asked is, "How would you like to see yourself?" and, "How much makeup do you feel comfortable wearing?" If the artist seems genuinely concerned about you as opposed to the products being sold and doesn't just give you the sales presentation as your makeup is being done, that's a good sign.

4. Check the artist's background: See if you can find out where they studied or who they trained under. Experience isn't everything but it's good information to have when making a decision between one professional and another.

In the long run, the worst that can happen when you see a makeup artist is that you won't like the work and then you can always wash it off. But the chances are that even if you don't like everything, you will most likely learn something from the experience; learning what you don't like is a part of a complete makeup education.

What To Discuss With Your Makeup Artist

1. How do you normally wear your makeup? Once you explain how much makeup you're used to wearing the artist can get an idea of how much makeup you will feel comfortable putting on. For example, if you are not used to wearing a foundation, then perhaps wearing only a mini-application of foundation will be best. If you are used to wearing only one eyeshadow, then perhaps it is best to move on to the two-color eye design before trying the back wedge or U-shaped crease color.

2. What is a typical or major color in your (seasonal) wardrobe? This will help decide which color direction to focus on. Quite frequently you will have both colors in your wardrobe, blue and yellow undertones, which may mean both makeup color families are necessary for you. If you are a beginner with makeup, start by choosing the color tones that are dominant in your closet.

3. How do you want to look? Or, what do you need this makeup for? This will give your artist an idea of how intense or conservatively you will want to wear your makeup. A desire for a more dramatic effect requires more color and defining; a casual, natural-looking makeup requires less. What do you need this makeup for? Work? Social event? If the makeup is for daytime business you will want to wear a more natural look. If it's for an evening out, and your clothes are more dramatic, then the makeup should be more dramatic.

4. Make sure it is okay with the artist that you can ask questions and get full explanations on what each item is for and how crucial it is for the overall makeup look. If after each item you're told that the makeup can't possibly survive without this essential step — do not buy a thing, you are getting a snow job, not a makeup lesson.

How To Deal With Cosmetic Salespeople

Keep these few things in mind next time you're perusing the cosmetic counters:

The cosmetic salesperson is not necessarily an authority. She is trained to sell a product, or, more accurately, she is trained to sell a lot of products. Be conscious that much of what you will be told are sales techniques and not information. Also, understand that none of that is the salesperson's fault; it is simply the way she earns her living.

No matter what you're being told, if for one moment you think you won't do it, don't buy it. You can reconsider and buy it the next time you're in the store. I promise you, the chances are they won't run out.

There is no such thing as "This product won't work without that product"; it sounds convincing but it isn't true.

The fancier or more scientific the claim or name sounds, regardless of price, you can be certain you will be wasting your money.

Do not approach or allow yourself to interact with a salesperson whom you feel intimidated by. That is true no matter what you are buying in life. If you don't feel comfortable you will make mistakes, either by buying too much or walking away and not buying what you need.

There is no truth to the superiority of one line over another. The superiority of a cosmetic is not in the brand name but in how the product works for you. One counter is the same as the next until you try the stuff on your face and price-compare.

They're Out To Get Our Children

I think this all started with the Barbie doll. That chesty little clothing monger whose outfits and makeup were eternally perfect. Her hair and makeup were always neatly in place no matter what we did to it. Barbie had to be handed down from sister to sister to sister before she ever showed any signs of wear and tear. Even when Ken came along, no matter what nasty things we made them do, her makeup never smeared and her hair was still in place.

Somewhere along the line the message starts very young that there is some mysterious beauty perfection that is attainable with a little added something that is not ours naturally. Television advertises it and our mothers unwittingly reinforce it. Our own moms sometimes make subtle comments on how we would look better with a little more of this thing or a lot more of the other thing. The idea that we looked fine just the way we were was rarely voiced. Maybe they were afraid we would grow up and go to work with scraped knees or dirty cheeks or maybe they were only projecting their own insecurities. How many of us have a clear picture of watching our own mothers spend endless hours tending to their hair, adjusting their lipstick, fastidiously applying their eye makeup and then exhaustedly wiping it off with cold cream at the end of the day. My mother's dark greasy eyes are as vivid an image to me as her perfectly made up face.

On the other hand, there were those of us who had moms that never wore makeup, who believed lipstick and blush were the devil's handmaidens. It happened sometime after we started getting our periods — out of nowhere we had the urge to play with makeup. We were probably testing our femininity and sexuality to see what it felt like being a woman. Once we began experimenting with makeup then the problems followed. Often we were punished for the thought of wanting to wear makeup even more than the actual red lips or blue lids we were caught with. Cosmetics made us look like sluts and that was intolerable. Wouldn't you know it — damned if we did and damned if we didn't.

As confusing as the messages were from our parents, the constant theme of not being okay the way we were or are, was and is a media standard for both ourselves and our children. The pulsating pictures on TV, in magazines and newspapers send us repeated images of happy, sexually satisfied, perfect-looking people. Those are powerful influences reminding us of what we need to do, or have, in order to be complete. Making us need something more than what we have is the most successful marketing tool of all.

This problem of being happy with ourselves just the way we are isn't only for us adults who have our own insecurities and lack of self-esteem to overcome. The issue is, do we want our children bombarded with the same disregard of human inner value and overemphasis on the artificially created exterior?

Children start very young dressing up in the images conveyed by the media and often we are helpless to stop it. Perhaps we as parents and teachers or friends forgot to praise the young people in our lives for being adored and loved for everything from the spilled milk to the straight A's; forgot to reassure them that what is precious about each of us is separate from what we do. Though, even if we had told our children, they might not have heard. The noise of our own lack of self-worth and the TV blasting in the background probably prevented the communication from getting through.

Perhaps the answer is awareness and an inner voice that is louder and stronger than what we are used to hearing. After all, what does Joan Collins really look like without her black eye makeup neatly in place? And if people are happy, it isn't because of their face, hair, figure or money, it's because their parents loved and praised them for being alive and didn't judge them as being bad or good. If we remind ourselves and the smaller ones around us of how wonderful we all are just the way we are, then the world would be a much safer place for our egos to live in. I vote for strong self-images, love of the natural inner and outer self that starts from very young and lasts till forever.

A Final Word — Makeup And Sexuality

Sex sells makeup and makeup is sexy. The first part of that statement is blatantly true. Pursed-lipped women, half-dressed men and beckoning looks adorn the ads selling cosmetics. The second part of that statement is equally true. When was the last time you saw a *Playboy* model posed with a freshly cleaned face? Yet the truth of it is, in person, makeup looks like makeup and when you are physically intimate with someone it gets all over the place. I wonder sometimes how intimate our makeup really allows us to be.

The way the media portrays it, makeup never gets in the way of an intimate moment: Lovers kiss and her makeup is still in place and he doesn't have any of it smeared all over his face. In a steamy shower scene a couple embraces under a cascading stream of water and her mascara doesn't run nor does the blush fade away. I see a shower and the first thing I want to do is wash my face; maybe I'm just not the romantic type. (Actually, it's more that I refuse to wear waterproof mascara and a shower or sweat makes my eye makeup run and that burns.)

The truth is that what we want is sometimes confused by our makeup and sometimes accentuated by it. There are times when I feel more sexy with a full makeup on and I forget all the problems I just conveyed. But, there are also times when the freshness of morning combined with a fresh natural me and my wonderful natural husband is more than sexy enough for both of us. I truly believe it is the inner voice that makes what we want a reality, not what the outside is saying.

For the last few words I have with you I'm not going to recommend ways for you to keep your makeup on throughout the night. Nor am I going to teach you how to touch up the smears after an active night together so he doesn't see you without your beautiful makeup on. Rather, I'm going to remind both of us that how sexy or powerful someone wants to be is only possible when they choose to be sexy or powerful. Clothing and makeup can portray certain images but, in the long run, what you believe to be the real you will always become apparent sooner or later. Makeup is a tool that with your own inner convictions and desires can be used to your best advantage. Going through the motions without that inner strength is, indeed, just going through the motions.

What do we want from our makeup? Of course that totally depends on us but I also think it depends on what we believe. We can feel sexy with or without makeup, it is totally up to us. As is true with any part of life, you usually get out of it exactly what you put into it.

Auxiliary Reading

A Consumer's Dictionary of Cosmetic Ingredients,
by Ruth Winter

Being Beautiful: Decide For Yourself, by Ralph Nader

Everything You Want To Know About Cosmetics,
by Toni Stabile

The Great American Skin Game, by Toni Stabile

Color Me Beautiful, by Carole Jackson

Dress The Body You Have To Look Like The Body You Want,
by Mary Duffy

All About Cosmetics, by Walter Klesper